# Online Learning Matters

## Extending your organisation's learning provision

Ali Close, Claudia Hesse, Eta De Cicco

©2009 National Institute of Adult Continuing Education
(England and Wales)
21 De Montfort Street
Leicester
LE1 7GE

Company registration no. 2603322
Charity registration no. 1002775

All rights reserved. No reproduction, copy or transmission of this publication may be made without the written permission of the publishers, save in accordance with the provisions of the Copyright, Designs and Patents Act 1988, or under the terms of any licence permitting copying issued by the Copyright Licensing Agency.

NIACE has a broad remit to promote lifelong learning opportunities for adults. NIACE works to develop increased participation in education and training, particularly for those who do not have easy access because of class, gender, age, race, language and culture, learning difficulties or disabilities, or insufficient financial resources.

You can find NIACE online at www.niace.org.uk

Cataloguing in Publication Data
A CIP record of this title is available from the British Library
Designed and typeset by Book Production Services, London
Printed and bound in the UK by Latimer Trend

ISBN: 978 1 86201 384 1

# Contents

**Introduction**   5

**Chapter 1**: Learning and the role of online delivery   9

**Chapter 2**: Designing the learning space   20

**Chapter 3**: Developing online provision   50

**Chapter 4**: Delivering learning online   74

**Chapter 5**: Sourcing and creating content   89

**Chapter 6**: Quality assurance and control   103

**Conclusion**   113

**Further information/references**   114

**Appendices**   116

Appendix A: Learning styles

Appendix B: Accessibility websites

Appendix C: Example of time taken by NIACE for initial course creation and delivery

Appendix D: Example assessment and tracking sheet for learners

Appendix E: Acceptable use policy for the NIACE Moodle

Appendix F: Guidelines for facilitating online chat

Appendix G: Contact record sheet

# Introduction

This publication has been written for community-based adult learning providers who want to develop and incorporate a cross-organisational approach to online learning and courses. The information within this publication also provides guidance to individuals who wish to include online methodologies within their teaching and learning.

Community-based adult learning is delivered in a variety of locations and involves an assortment of learning arrangements, styles and learning methods. The learning can be accredited, non-accredited, part time or full time. It is not always based on courses and can include events such as open days and celebrations, and activities involving learning such as producing a video or newsletter.

The main characteristic of adult learning is its diversity. Learners vary in age, social and ethnic background, experience and ability. Adult learners' purposes in learning are many and include:

- exploring new interests

- meeting other people

- getting a qualification

- keeping fit, active and alert

- dealing with life transitions or crises

- helping or keeping up with children

- finding out about new technology

- acquiring skills to use in a particular situation.

Technology has become a part of our daily lives. We use cash machines to withdraw money, internet banking to manage our finances, and mobile phones to be contactable around the clock – and some to access the internet. We listen to music and record photos and video, buy goods and services over the internet, use digital set-top boxes to watch television or to customise and record television programmes, and digital players to listen to our music and watch videos wherever we go. These are just a few examples of how technology has permeated our lives.

Online technology, especially, has revolutionised how we find information, plan our travels and interact with the world around us. A natural conclusion seems to be that online technology also has an impact on how we learn.

Given the variety of learning arrangements and locations for adult learning, the online environment presents another opportunity for adult learning providers to engage learners in new and exciting ways. Online learning offers adult learners greater flexibility to learn at their own pace, at any time and in locations of their choice.

We (the authors) have drawn upon our own experiences of developing and delivering online learning within NIACE, and on the practice of other education and training providers. By describing how to deliver facilitated online or blended courses from an organisational viewpoint, we also cover all the elements necessary for other options such as developing and delivering self-study online courses, online learning activities (one-off sessions and online elements to support face-to-face sessions) and online conference provision. Throughout the publication, we invite you at intervals to reflect on your own situation and how you can incorporate some of the aspects explored into your own plan for online learning provision. Each chapter also provides you with a checklist to help you plan your organisation's online learning provision.

We begin our journey in Chapter 1 by exploring the concepts of learning and online learning and the potential role of online methodologies to extend and enhance learning provision. Different pedagogical approaches and theories are also considered in Chapter 1.

Chapters 2, 3 and 4 depict a process that moves from designing the learning space (in Chapter 2), through to developing your online provision (Chapter 3) and finally to delivering learning within an online environment (Chapter 4).

An in-depth look at the type of content learning providers may want to use and where this content might come from is covered in Chapter 5. Formative and summative evaluation of learning is also included within this chapter.

Finally, Chapter 6 considers the factors involved in ensuring and sustaining the quality of your online provision.

Where applicable, we provide illustrations and examples of practice to support the key messages within the publication. These examples are included to help you develop a quality-assured approach to online learning provision.

# Chapter 1
# Learning and the role of online delivery

> 'For teachers, lecturers and tutors it [online learning] means easy and efficient ways of keeping in touch, giving feedback on students' progress, and managing marking and assessment. [...] With more flexible e-learning resources available online, teachers can adapt the curriculum to their learners' needs and interests. Technology is the key to personalised learning.'
>
> Ruth Kelly in Harnessing technology: Transforming Learning and Children's Services, DfES, 2005

## What the research says about learning

To grasp the concept of online learning, it may help to first step back and look at learning in general. Numerous theories seek to define learning and how we learn. The research evidence about how adults learn is conflicting. Knowles (1980, 1984) suggests that adults learn differently from young children and want to be more self-directed in their learning. Knowles admits that despite wanting to be more independent, adults may lack an understanding of what this entails. Adults need guidance on the processes of learning.

Life experiences are critical to the adult learning process according to Taylor, Marienau, and Fiddler (2000) because adults are more likely than children to bring to learning greater life experiences. Robinson (1992) found that adults on distance learning programmes often used life experiences to complete their assignments. However, Brookfield (1995) and Yonge (1984) both suggest that, although important, life experiences alone do not define adult learning, and that the manner in which adults and children learn is basically the same. If Brookfield and Yonge are right, then current theories of how we learn apply both to children and adults.

Two particular approaches to learning may be of interest to those working with adult learners within an online environment: the European Commission's work on learning, and research by Mayes and de Freitas (2007).

The European Commission suggests that intention to learn and the context in which learning takes place should define learning, and provides the following definitions:

- **Formal learning** consists of learning that occurs within an organised and structured context (formal education; in-company training) and is designed as learning. It may lead to certification. Formal learning is intentional from the learner's perspective.

- **Non-formal learning** consists of learning embedded in planned activities that are *not explicitly designated as learning*, but which contain an important learning element. Non-formal learning is intentional from the learner's point of view.

- **Informal learning** is defined as learning resulting from daily life activities related to work, family or leisure. It is often referred to as accidental learning. Informal learning is not structured in terms of learning objectives, learning time or learning support. Typically, it does not lead to certification. Informal learning *may be intentional*, but in most cases it is non-intentional.

Source: Communiqué: Making a European area of lifelong learning a reality, European Commission, Brussels, 2001

This categorisation of learning shows that what we often understand as education and training is, in fact, formal learning. Yet, other learning does take place in all kinds of situations within daily life, both at work and at home, and this is particularly true within community-based adult learning.

Mayes and de Freitas (2007) conclude in a report for the Joint Information Systems Committee (JISC) that most theories about how we learn can be put into one of three distinct groups, which are learning as:

- activity (empiricist)
- achieving understanding (cognitive)
- social practice (situative).

## Learning as activity

This perspective is built upon the belief that learning is about forming and strengthening associations between ideas, thoughts and information. Knowledge and skills need to be broken down into small units, with the easier units taught first and eventually leading to the more complex units.

Behaviourism is an example of this category – the learner plays a passive role in learning and simply responds to positive or negative reinforcement. This approach to learning led to the development of computer-based training and software packages to teach routine skills, such as those produced for health and safety.

## Learning as achieving understanding

Here, learning is about making sense of the world and our experiences. Learning is seen as the outcome of new experiences interacting with what we already know, building knowledge and understanding.

Constructivism is one theory under this category. Learners actively create their own subjective reality based on personal experiences. The concept of the reflective practitioner can also sit here.

## Learning as social practice

This theory assumes that the social and cultural setting in which learning occurs has an important influence on learning. As Mayes and de Freitas explain, '*this view of learning focuses on the way knowledge is distributed socially*'. This theory therefore builds upon the notion of learning through social development.

Problem-based learning and communities of practice are examples of this type of theory and suggest that learners should receive knowledge within the places and activities where they normally use it.

We will refer to these three groupings of learning theories and how they relate to online learning in Chapter 2: *Designing the learning space*.

## **Learning with technology**

Learning takes places in many different settings and can take many forms, as shown by the differentiation between formal, informal and non-formal learning earlier in this chapter. Technology allows us to support these different forms of learning.

Technology has been used in learning for over 30 years, mainly in the commercial training field for what was known as computer-based training or computer-assisted learning. Online learning is a more recent phenomenon.

We can approach the use of technology to support learning as a continuum, encompassing a broad range of activities across a spectrum. The spectrum (see Figure 1) spans from e-learning – the use of any technology to facilitate and enhance learning – through blended learning, which combines face-to-face delivery with online activities, to learning that is delivered entirely online.

**Figure 1:** *Learning with technology*

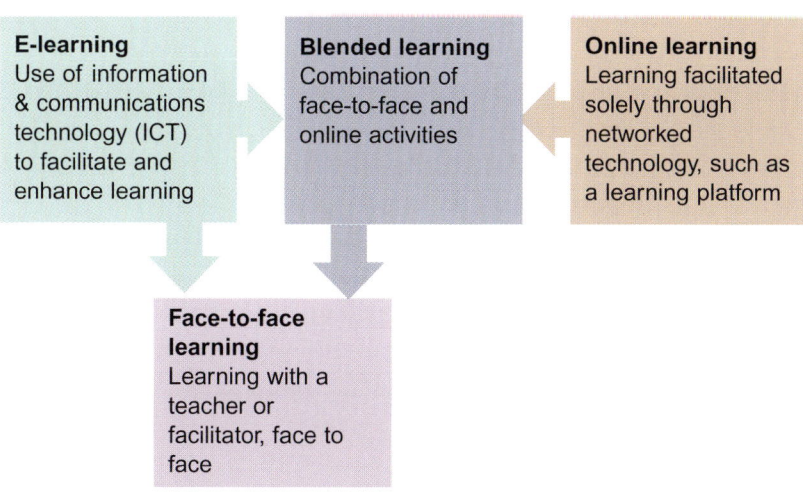

Sometimes the terms e-learning and online learning are used interchangeably. However, to understand the different applications of technology for learning, we will distinguish between these terms. Both online learning and e-learning use technology to support learning; however, online learning uses networked technology to deliver the learning, while e-learning integrates technology to facilitate learning, but does not necessarily include online delivery. Combining online elements with face-to-face delivery is referred to as blended learning.

**Online learning**
Learning facilitated solely through networked technology and delivered via a learning platform, an intranet or the internet.

**E-learning**
Learning facilitated and supported by information and communications technology (ICT).

**Blended learning**
Online elements combined or blended with traditional forms of learning such as those that take place in classrooms and learning centres.

Online learning has increased significantly, both in quantity and importance, since internet connectivity became available to a large proportion of the population.

## The role of online delivery

As technology becomes part of our daily lives, online technology naturally gains in importance in how we learn. We can learn using the technology that we use in our daily lives for many other purposes. Also, using online technology in learning can help us become more knowledgeable and confident in using it across different aspects of our lives, including in the workplace. However, this value is limited: a learning offer is only as good as the pedagogy that underpins it.

Advocates of online learning often list many of the benefits that online learning can offer. These include:

- enhancing learner-to-learner and faculty-to-learner communication
- enabling learner-centered teaching approaches
- providing 24/7 accessibility to learning – any time, any place
- providing just-in-time methods to assess and evaluate learners' progress
- overcoming the digital divide and widening participation.

### Enhancing learner-to-learner and faculty-to-learner communication

Because of the nature of online technology and multimedia, online learning offers an opportunity to design rich, differentiated and motivating learning experiences. The emergence of networking websites such as Facebook [http://www.facebook.com] has the potential to add a range of online communication tools to the online learning context. However, if applied badly, such tools can repel potential learners and have an adverse effect.

### Enabling learner-centered teaching approaches

Online learning can be an opportunity for opening up learning to more learners and, if designed effectively, can provide a better learning experience. As online technology is just a technology, it depends on us to use it effectively. It is crucial to design an online learning offer with the potential learner at the centre of the planning process. The pedagogy, along with the physical and cultural access to the technology, determines how successful the learning offer can be.

### Any time, any place

Advocates for online learning point out that it allows us to learn at any time, in any place, because of the nature of technology. This aspect of online learning can help overcome geographical and time constraints. By moving learning out of a classroom into our homes or workplaces, it potentially becomes more accessible to a wider group of learners.

In a world in which many of us work unsociable and longer hours, the potential of online learning becomes more significant. People who would be excluded from further learning and training because of their working hours can access learning at a time and in a place suitable to their needs. Online learning can also support employers who need to further develop and train their staff: it can offer a way of working with time or geographical constraints to develop a skilled workforce.

### Providing just-in-time methods to assess and evaluate learners' progress

Online learning can be seen as another tool in the toolbox for facilitating learning. Its ability to offer learning at a time and in a place of learners' choosing means that online learning can provide not only just-in-time learning and support, but also just-in-time assessment and feedback.

## Overcoming the digital divide and widening participation

The term digital divide is widely used to describe the unequal access by some members of society to ICT, and the unequal acquisition of related skills. Groups often discussed in the context of a digital divide include socio-economic (rich/poor), racial (majority/minority), generational (young/old) or geographical (urban/rural).[1]

> "The culture of ICT [...] is young, white middle-class and male; precisely the narrow attributes of the traditional adult learning base the government are so keen to move beyond. Many of the technologies used to deliver learning (the Internet etc.) are not necessarily dominant or familiar technology with the working class, older, female, ethnic learner."
>
> Gorard and Selwyn (2000)

The statement quoted above is taken from a paper written in 2000. However, studies need to be undertaken to establish whether the digital divide has changed. The widespread use of new generation digital televisions, cheaper broadband connections (or in some cases free internet connection as part of a phone or digital television contract), cheaper computers and widespread access to the internet in public places may have changed the situation significantly. Access to the internet through a variety of technologies in different settings may have lifted cultural barriers and supported more members of society to gain access to technology and develop relevant skills for using technology effectively. However, sufficient public access to computers and the internet must be provided, otherwise the divide may not narrow but deepen.

We are all different, and we all learn in different ways. Online learning approaches add another option for how we can learn. It can offer a safe environment for learners who prefer to avoid

---

[1] http://en.wikipedia.org/wiki/Digital_divide

learning in a face-to-face classroom situation with other learners. Online learning can offer anonymity, and thus might help overcome some learners' fears.

## Use of learning styles within online delivery

The research into how we learn has also led to the concept of learning styles. However, the impact that learning styles have on the success of online delivery is uncertain. Some researchers believe that learning can be enhanced if the various learning styles are taken into account.

Online learning methods are often less guided and more self-directed than other methods. Some researchers argue that learners who prefer direct instruction may get lost because of their lack of ability to adjust to the learning environment, and that this can result in less successful learning experiences (Chen, 2002; Daniels and Moore, 2000; Ford and Chen, 2000). The researchers argue that certain types of learners can be disoriented and may miss information when they are overloaded by the non-linear presentation of information in web-based environments. Dede (1996) supports this view and suggests that the relationships among the individual pieces of information provided online need to be made explicit.

There are also those who downplay the importance of learning styles. King (1998) states that while learning styles may affect learning, equally significant is *'matching the language and design of the site to the skills and needs of its intended audience'*. Palloff and Pratt (1999) reported that students with any learning style can learn effectively online. Finally, findings from a study by Oh and Lim (2005) conclude that only a few important variables affect the ability of learners to learn online. These factors are learners':

- attitudes to learning
- pre-existing topic knowledge and understanding

- levels of competency in using computer technology, and their experiences with online learning.

In view of the findings by Oh and Lim, you should consider the above factors in your initial assessment of learners. This is particularly important if the online session or course is to stand alone, and if learners will receive no human support or engage in any face-to-face activity.

To address the many and varied learning styles, it is good practice – both online and offline – to present your content and deliver your activities in a variety of ways, and include appropriate use of images, animation, video, audio and simulation.

A multitude of tools approach the subject of learning styles from different perspectives. A few of the most well-known tools are outlined in Appendix A: 'Learning styles'. If you are interested in learning styles, an internet-based search will yield many results.

More background information on pedagogy and learning theories is also available on the NIACE Staff development e-learning centre (SDELC) website [http://www.sdelc.co.uk]. If you are new to this site, you will need to register. Registration is free and enables you to keep copies of personal notes and any completed or partially completed forms, and track your continuing professional development (CPD) through learning plans and reflective journals. Once you have logged in to the site, go to **Common modules** > **Getting started**.

### Pause and reflect

- What are your experiences of how adults learn?
- Which of the three learning approaches identified by Mayes and de Freitas, in your opinion, contribute to good teaching?

## Checklist: Your delivery approach

You can use this checklist to help you plan your online learning provision in your own organisation.

|  | Yes | No | Perhaps |
|---|---|---|---|
| **What type of online learning do I want to provide?** | | | |
| Formal | | | |
| Non-formal | | | |
| Informal | | | |
| A combination of all three | | | |
| **Am I considering using a particular pedagogical approach?** | | | |
| Associationist/Instructional Systems Design | | | |
| Cognitive/Constructivist | | | |
| Situative perspective | | | |
| Other | | | |
| A combination of all three | | | |
| None | | | |
| **Am I considering catering for a particular learning style?** | | | |
| Kolb | | | |
| Honey and Mumford | | | |
| Felder and Silverman | | | |
| Myers Briggs | | | |
| Bloom | | | |
| Gagné | | | |
| Race | | | |
| Skinner | | | |
| Other | | | |
| None | | | |

# Chapter 2
# Designing the learning space

In Chapter 1: *Learning and the role of online delivery*, we introduced Mayes and de Freitas's three groups of learning approaches: learning as activity, learning as achieving understanding, and learning as social practice. While the three categories are not exhaustive, they do represent an overview that encompasses the various learning theories. This publication will use these groupings to explore online provision.

If you decide to develop online activities within your organisation, and are starting from scratch, you will face the task of designing your learning space. The design of your online provision should preferably form part of your overall curriculum design processes, since you need to decide how your online activities will fit into your other learning provision. This is also true of your quality assurance and quality control system. You should consider the quality of your online learning within your organisation's general quality assurance systems.

Designing an online space is very similar to designing a face-to-face curriculum, except you now have a number of technological tools to add to your teaching and learning arsenal (see Figure 2). Once you know who your learners are and the intended learning outcomes, you need to decide:

- your mode(s) of delivery – how you will break down the learning and how the online learning space and materials will be organised

- the nature of the content and materials you will use and what activities you will provide, including feedback and assessment activities

- the type and amount of support you will provide for learners
- what technology you will use.

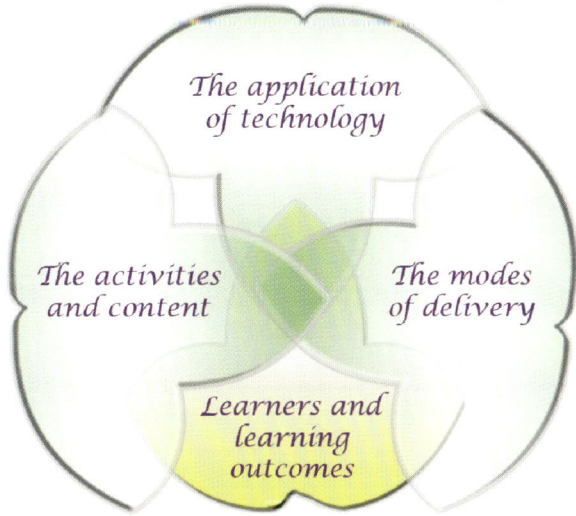

**Figure 2:** *Designing online learning*

Three further issues cut across all these elements: accessibility, assessment (see Chapter 5: *Sourcing and creating content*) and quality assurance (see Chapter 6: *Quality assurance and control*).

## Learners and learning outcomes

If they have access to a computer and any necessary software, your learners can participate in an online course or event irrespective of their geographic location.

Obviously, if you are running a blended course, the participants may need to travel to the face-to-face elements, which may influence your catchment area. You could consider offering only one face-to-face induction event and delivering the remainder of the course online, or even offering those learners who cannot travel to your face-to-face induction an option to access an induction online. Potentially, therefore, you could attract learners from all over the UK and even from outside the UK.

The downside of attracting learners from outside the UK is that you may need to make provision for different time zones when scheduling the course, and for varying language skills and cultural differences. (For example, what are classed as acceptable comments in one culture may be considered offensive in others.)

Find out all you can about your intended audience before you start planning your online space. You need to consider who your target audiences are before you make decisions about the design, content or approach of your online learning provision.

- **Age range**: Take account of the age range of your intended learners when developing your content and activities. For example, content for young children may need to be presented in a different way to that provided for some adult learners.

- **Culture**: Be sensitive to cultural differences and the possibility of different language skills among learners.

- **Learning needs**: Find out whether any of your learners require additional support and assistance, both educational and technical. You may need to adjust the technology, content and delivery to take account of issues such as visual impairment, deafness, dyslexia and motor impairment.

- **Learning styles**: Try to incorporate a variety of learning styles within your online design so that learners with different learning styles all benefit.

- **Expectation and motivation**: Make the nature of your course and its learning outcomes clear to learners from the start. For example, is the online provision accredited or does it lead to a qualification, or do you expect learners to participate out of general interest and for self-improvement?

- **Possible constraints**: Ensure that you are aware of any barriers that learners face in accessing provision. Your learners may be trying to fit the course or event around work, family or other commitments.

Once you have undertaken some sort of needs analysis or initial assessment of your intended learners, you can develop your learning outcomes. Learning outcomes are statements that identify what learners will know, understand or be able to do as a result of a learning activity. Learning outcomes are useful because they:

- inform learners what is expected of them

- help teachers and facilitators to focus on what they want learners to understand, know or do at the end of the learning intervention.

> **Pause and reflect**
>
> The questions to ask at this initial stage of the design process are:
>
> - Who are the learners that I want to attract and will be delivering to?
>
> - What do I want learners to know, understand and/or do by the end of the intervention?

## Modes of delivery

Once you have decided who your learners are and what their learning outcomes will be, you can consider the next stage of the design process: the mode(s) of delivery.

It is widely believed that online learning (and indeed, learning in general) is more effective if it is delivered in small chunks, each lasting about 20 minutes. It may therefore be worth breaking your online course or event down into small, manageable sections. This aligns with the trend in the UK to unitise the curriculum. Unitisation (also referred to as modularisation) is used to describe programmes of study built up from smaller units or modules (that is, small chunks of learning). Learners can gain credit for any units studied, and can combine certain units together to form a qualification.

You should ensure that each section is self-contained – that is, that it includes all the content and activities required to meet the overarching course learning outcome. Whether you break your materials down into sections or not, it is important to provide an overview so that learners can see what the course or event entails.

At this point, you also need to explore how you will deliver these chunks of learning. The options include:

- a fully facilitated online course, learning session or event

- a fully facilitated blended course, learning session or event

- a self-study (non-facilitated) online course, learning session or event

- non-facilitated online content and activities to enhance delivery of a face-to-face course, session or event. The NIACE Staff development e-learning centre (SDELC) website [http://www.sdelc.co.uk] (as mentioned in Chapter 1) is an example of a non-facilitated self-study area.

If you decide to offer a facilitated option, that is, you will provide some form of human support for the learning, it is probable that the staff involved in the project will require online learning skills. You have two main choices with regard to staff development:

- Take a localised approach and leave staff to develop their skills organically – although even this approach may require funding, time and support.

- Take an organisation-wide approach and consider embedding online skills as part of your training provision for most or all staff.

With both approaches, members of staff will need access to appropriate IT and to have IT support in place. Chapter 4: 'Delivering learning online' looks at online learning skills in more detail.

> **Pause and reflect**
>
> The overarching questions you need to ask at this stage of the design process are:
>
> - What type of course am I developing?
>
> - How will I break down the required learning into small, manageable chunks?

## Application of technology

When designing an online learning offer, it is most important to think about the learner, the pedagogy (learning approach) and your learning objectives first, and the technology second. Online technologies offer many opportunities; however, you can only exploit these opportunities if technologies are used appropriately. Therefore, approach your decisions about which technology to use by reflecting on *how* you might apply the technology to achieve your learning objectives.

Table 1 outlines a number of examples of how you might apply current technologies to a learning approach. Since technology is always changing and evolving, the examples are by no means exhaustive.

It is important to remember that the learning approaches (as discussed in Chapter 1: 'Learning and the role of online delivery') are not mutually exclusive. Effective learning results from combining all three approaches and also combining different technological tools from all the categories to help you achieve the learning objectives. Definitions and descriptions of the tools mentioned in the table below can be found in Chapter 3: 'Developing online provision'.

| Learning approach | Main focus of approach | Examples of technologies that could support the approach |
| --- | --- | --- |
| Learning as activity | The topic and subject matter | Technologies that focus on the topic: computer-based training, including instructional videos and audio, digital how-to and step-by-step guides, small, self-contained chunks of learning content (learning objects), e assessment and quiz software, and some computer-based interactive tutorials. |
| Learning as achieving understanding | Thinking about learning, not about the topic<br><br>Building on past experiences | Technologies that encourage dialogue and reflection: chat facilities, discussion boards, e-portfolios, blogs, text messaging, wikis, audio and video messaging, audio and video conferencing, mobile phones. |
| Learning as social practice | Building communities of practice<br><br>Collaborative professional development<br><br>Knowledge and skills sharing | Technologies that represent communities of practice in an online environment or that facilitate sharing of knowledge and skill: virtual worlds, simulations, computer games, collaborative tools such as wikis, interactive whiteboards, audio and video messaging, audio and video conferencing, computer-based interactive tutorials. |

**Table 1:** *Applying technology to learning*

In general, online technologies fall into two main categories: asynchronous and synchronous.

> **Asynchronous**
> These tools are designed to enable contributions from and collaboration with participants who are not necessarily all online at the same time.
>
> Discussion forums and wikis are examples of asynchronous tools, and enable learners to keep in touch and work collaboratively. These forms of computer-mediated communication (CMC) are particularly advantageous when delivering online courses.
>
> The use of asynchronous tools within your online course allows facilitators and learners to participate at a time to suit them. Learners also have the opportunity to think about what they want to say and to consider peer and facilitator responses before posting messages. Or, as with a face-to-face discussion, learners can simply read the messages and not contribute.
>
> **Synchronous**
> These tools are designed to enable contributions from and collaboration with participants who are online at the same time – i.e. in real time.
>
> Chat rooms and instant messaging are examples of synchronous tools, and enable learners and facilitators to communicate in small groups or on a one-to-one basis.

Knowing whether the tool you intend to use is synchronous or asynchronous is important, because the content you develop or use may need to be adapted depending on whether it will be delivered live or placed online so that each learner accesses it at different times.

Chapter 3: *Developing online provision* looks at asynchronous and synchronous CMC tools in more detail.

## The learning platform

Your final consideration with regard to the technology is what mechanism you will use to enable your learners to access the learning – your learning platform. But first, what do we mean by learning platform?

A learning platform is the delivery and administration mechanism that delivers the learning content and activities to the learner. At its most extreme, this definition could be taken to include using a web browser and web-based content on a CD-ROM, DVD or other removable storage device. But in reality, learning platforms are much more than this.

> **Definition of a learning platform**
>
> The term learning platform covers a variety of tools, all of which, used together, support elements of online learning in some way.
>
> A learning platform usually brings together three main types of tool or system:
>
> - Content creation: Tools/systems that enable the delivery of electronic learning content, whether this content is written in house or imported from other commercial packages.
> - Communication and collaboration: Tools/systems that support communication and collaborative working, for example email, discussion lists and wikis.
> - Management of learning: Any tools/systems that support the management of the teaching and learning process, such as those for enrolment, tracking of progress, and formative or summative assessment.
>
> Within education and training environments three terms are commonly used to describe learning platforms:
>
> - Virtual Learning Environment (VLE)
> - Website/web portal
> - Intranet.
>
> Adapted from e-Learning Professional Development (Unit 4)
> [http://www.learningtechnologies.ac.uk/ecpd/lister/listing_04.htm]

We will look at the concept of and options for Virtual Learning Environments (VLE) first, and then we will briefly consider other learning platform options.

## Virtual Learning Environments

A VLE helps you build a sustainable model of online learning provision within your organisation.

Most VLEs feature some or all of the following:

| Core function | Practical application |
| --- | --- |
| Content publication<br><br>Content management | Tutors are able to upload existing learning and teaching materials to the system.<br><br>Tutors are able to create learning and teaching materials within the system.<br><br>Tutors control the release of materials – ie although a file is loaded into the system, the tutor may choose not to make it public to learners until a certain date. |
| Communication and collaboration (bulletin boards, chat rooms, shared whiteboards, course calendars, wikis, databases and assessment facilities) | Course members may communicate. (Because the tools are within the learning platform, communication is restricted to course members.) |
| Management of learning | Learners are enrolled online.<br><br>Grading, learner tracking and page tracking reports are available.<br><br>Most VLEs offer the ability to track the pages visited by individual users and to offer data on the most popular pages, scores from quizzes, etc. |

| Tracking and assessment | Formative and summative assessments may be undertaken. Most VLEs feature simple assessment tools – usually a variation on a multiple-choice questionnaire. |
|---|---|
| Customisation | It is possible to pick appropriate tools for each course. VLEs usually offer tutors the ability to edit the appearance and layout of their courses. It is possible to integrate the VLE with other learner management systems within an organisation. |

Note: Further explanations of the tools in this table can be found under 'Communication and collaboration' in Chapter 3: *Developing online provision*.

NIACE uses the Moodle (Modular Object Oriented Dynamic Learning Environment) learning environment. This open source software application was designed especially for providing internet-based online courses. (Open source software is provided free of charge, and is also known as freeware.)

Moodle was designed to apply the following principles when creating a learning offer:

- All of us are potential teachers as well as learners – in a true collaborative environment, we are both.
- We learn particularly well from the act of creating or expressing something for others to see (from teaching others).
- We learn a lot by just observing the activity of our peers.
- By understanding the contexts of others, we can teach in a more transformational way.
- A learning environment needs to be flexible and adaptable, so that it can quickly respond to the needs of the participants within it.

Moodle aims to promote social constructionism, an approach that focuses on learning through understanding, although the principles on which Moodle is designed also cross a number of Mayes and de Freitas's groupings (See Chapter 1: *Learning and the role of online delivery*). It is important to note that while Moodle was designed according to these principles, not all users of Moodle apply them when designing an online learning session or event.

The main advantages of a VLE are that it offers an integrated learning platform and enables tutors and facilitators control of their individual 'virtual' areas and courses. It also provides a safe and secure learning environment for learners – you can set each course area to be accessed solely by those participating in the course and its facilitators.

Several commercial and open source VLEs are available, most of which offer the functions described in the table above. Those who are obtaining and installing a VLE for the first time will also find a wealth of information, advice and guidance on the internet.

Questions to consider when looking at the various VLE options are:

- How could this VLE be used within my organisation?

- Would the use of this VLE improve our learning provision?

- Will members of staff and potential learners be able to use this VLE easily and with little or no support?

- What other support might I need – for example staff development, technical support?

- Is there potential to develop this VLE in the future, for example to integrate it with existing systems?

- Will this VLE be cost effective?

We will look at how you can use some of the functions and tools found in a VLE in Chapter 3: 'Developing online provision'. Now we will take a quick look at other learning platform options you may like to consider for some or all of your online learning provision.

Note that many of the tools found within learning platforms – discussion forums, chat rooms, wikis, upload tools (software that enables you to send data to a website) and assessment and quiz tools – were around long before VLEs. Therefore, it is possible to assemble a home-grown web-based learning platform using tools found on the internet, often at a fraction of the cost of buying a commercial VLE. The downside is that this assemblage is more difficult to integrate into your other organisational systems, and the tools may not be able to share data with each other.

## Websites/web portals

Some websites or web portals require learners to register and log on to access online provision.

The main issue with using a website as your learning platform is one of scale. If your online provision becomes successful, learners' and tutors' needs and expectations grow, and simple websites become increasingly difficult to maintain.

In order to better manage large websites and to enable staff who may not have high levels of technical skill to publish content on a website, you can use a content management system (CMS) – software to automate the process of creating, publishing and maintaining content on a website. A CMS structures web-based information resources such as text, images and documents so that they can be stored, published and more easily updated. A CMS normally separates the page design (how your pages look) from the actual content (what your pages contain). The key goal of a CMS is to increase integration and automation of the processes that support efficient and effective internet delivery.

If you simply want a straightforward method of publishing your learning materials on the internet or intranet for your learners to access, then a CMS is an option. However, a CMS is a significant expense – even free open source content management systems require installation and technical support. Generally, it is larger organisations, with many employees generating large amounts of content that invest in such technologies.

Many organisations struggle to maintain their websites, resulting in out-of-date material and poor control over design and navigation. A lack of authority and control, and sometimes the constriction of the individual responsible for managing the website (the web master), or even a web team, can lead to bottlenecks. The diverse requirements for adult learning resources and the lack of funding to employ a dedicated web and multimedia specialist may also affect the creation and maintenance of a successful website.

*Intranet*

An intranet is a private computer network, similar to the World Wide Web, but accessible only to an organisation and its staff. It may or may not incorporate some form of content management system, and often requires users to log on.

In the teaching and learning context, intranets are currently used to provide content to support face-to-face classes. But they can also provide more sophisticated features such as interactive notice boards and discussion forums, so it would be wrong to see intranets as a poor relation of integrated systems such as VLEs.

Intranets can be, and are, used to greatly enhance teaching and learning, and, with the arrival of increasingly useable intranet site-development and management tools, intranets are well within the price range of educational organisations that do not have a dedicated web developer.

## Shared folders

Shared folders provide a simple way to share files over an organisation's computer network or intranet. It is relatively easy to set up user access rights so that, for example, learners can read files but not change them. Shared folders can be quick to set up, and may be easier to implement than putting files on a website or intranet.

Products like Microsoft Exchange Server [http://www.microsoft.com/exchange/default.mspx] provide a much more sophisticated version of the shared folders concept, enabling you to send and receive email and other forms of interactive communication through any computer network that is using the Microsoft Outlook® email package. The Exchange Server's collaboration features allow you to share and edit information such as address lists, meeting schedules and the content of mailboxes.

## Storage devices

You can use low cost storage devices such as CD-ROMs, DVDs and removable memory devices to distribute learning materials to your learners. However, if you use these storage devices to deliver your content and standalone activities, you must find other ways to interact with and support your learners online, and for them to submit any assignment work or evidence of learning.

## A final word on learning platforms

Whatever learning platform you decide to use, it should be simple, straightforward, easy to use and consistent. Learners should know exactly what to do and where they are, and should not have to hunt for buttons to press or tools to use. You should incorporate a consistent approach to your navigation, on-screen controls and hyperlinks, with information buttons and icons consistently appearing in the same place on every screen.

Always try to create your online space as if you were the learner. Engaging learners in all the steps of your online design, development and delivery is always a good idea – they may well come up with new ideas and useful suggestions. Whenever possible, test out your online provision with a pilot group of learners before you go live.

**Pause and reflect**

The questions to ask at this stage of the design process are:

- Which technology tools, including a learning platform, are currently available to you?

- How might you use these tools – and others – to deliver your online provision?

## Activities and content

Having decided on your approaches to delivery, you now need to consider how you are going to create and organise your materials.

When writing your content for online delivery, you must bear in mind that your learners may use the materials in isolation, and so the structure of the materials and activities and the path through them must be clear and unambiguous.

A variety of software tools are available to enable you to create learning content. You may already have preferred content creation tools available within your organisation, or you may word process your content and then send it to a technical or content authoring department or organisation to convert it into a format to deliver to the learner. Chapter 5: *Sourcing and creating content* looks at various content creation options in more detail.

When deciding the nature of the content for your learning sessions, consider these three inter-related criteria:

- How you intend the learning materials to be delivered

- Whether the materials need to stand alone or form part of a face-to-face activity (ie part of a blended activity)

- The degree of human support that you will make available to learners as they access the content.

## How will the learning materials be delivered?

There is a relationship between the nature of the learning content and the mode(s) of delivery. If you have begun to think about the type of content you want to develop, you should already have decided, as part of your curriculum design process (see *Modes of delivery*, above), the relationship between the synchronous and asynchronous elements of your course and the elements' contribution to your learning outcomes.

Whether it is acceptable to use the same digital content for both synchronous and asynchronous delivery depends on how you envisage the facilitator and learner interacting with the material. For example, a tutor has produced a digital presentation for a small group of learners about a specific topic. If the tutor delivers this presentation live online (synchronous delivery), during delivery, the tutor will add a wealth of information to the content on the slides. If the tutor intends to put the presentation online after completing the live delivery, the additional information that the tutor provides during the live session must be captured and included.

In some cases, the software used to deliver a live session can record the session. You can then make this recording available for learners.

If you do not record the session, the tutor needs to add audio or comprehensible notes to the slides, or produce separate digital content to complement the presentation and help learners make sense of it. Failure to provide this information could result in those accessing the presentation outside the live session failing to meet the intended learning outcomes. This could affect learners who miss the live session, as well as those who revisit the presentation after the live session.

Given the conflicting evidence about learning styles, it may be worth designing the content for your session so that learners can interact with it in a number of ways: via images, animation, video, audio and text. In this way, you allow for different learner preferences in how they access information – just in case. But be careful and do not add multimedia just for its own sake. Multimedia has no value unless it helps the content meet the needs of learners and the learning outcomes of the session. And remember, the more complex the interactivity, the more likely it is that the content developers will need advanced technical skills, and the more costly the process.

## Will the learning materials stand alone or form part of a face-to-face activity?

As part of the curriculum design process, you will also have decided whether the online element will stand alone – ie no face-to-face delivery is involved – or whether it will form a part of a face-to-face activity or course. You will need to consider who may access the content and how your learners may interact with any material you produce.

It is common practice on the internet to publish materials that were delivered during or prepared for a face-to-face activity, like a classroom session or conference, online. The resources are often published without any amendments.

If your learners attended the face-to-face activity, they may benefit from revisiting the materials online. However, if your learners did not attend the event, then placing the content online with no contextualisation or changes may not achieve the learning outcomes you had intended. Many presentations on the internet fail to provide this added-value information, which makes them little use to anyone who did not attend the original event. You may need to add audio, extra explanatory notes, online activities or assessments to the online content to help people make sense of it.

Equally, consider the relationship between the materials you produce in paper form for the face-to-face event and the online content. Does one depend on the other? Do you want the materials to contribute to different aspects of your learning outcomes?

If you intend from the start that the content will stand alone and have no face-to-face element to contextualise it, it is even more important to wrap it up with enough detail to enable learners to benefit. Unless you know the intended audience well, do not assume that its members can learn independently. This is true even if the intended audience is adult learners.

Therefore, before you publish materials online that you used during a face-to-face delivery, consider:

- why you are making the materials available online

- who the intended audience are: people who attended or did not attend your face-to-face sessions?

- how an individual might interact differently with the content online as opposed to during a live, face-to-face session

- whether there is any relationship between the materials you produce in paper form during the face-to-face event and the online content.

You may find (especially in the early parts of an online course) that you need to repeat instructions on how to use the materials or navigate the online space. This support will help learners become comfortable with their learning environment, and should not be seen as unnecessary.

The activities you choose to provide for your learners should be closely linked to the materials and content you provide.

Your content should be concise. Many online courses contain more information than learners can digest. You can add an option for further reading or exploration at the end of each section or module for those learners who want to research the topic in more depth.

If you use multimedia techniques, such as incorporating images, audio, video or animation, the techniques should be relevant and appropriate, and support the learning. Including a variety of approaches will help keep your learners engaged and motivated. Remember that you need to provide alternative ways of accessing the learning for accessibility reasons (see *Accessibility* section below).

Depending on the overall aims of your online learning course or event, you can take a variety of approaches, using a mixture of different technology tools to cater for an assortment of learning styles and methods (see Chapter 1: 'Learning and the role of online delivery'). Table 1 earlier in this chapter outlines some of the current technologies that you can apply to learning.

## How much human support will you provide?

The degree of human support provided from a facilitator or tutor to accompany the materials also determines the level of detail you need to include in your online content. The resources you use may differ in complexity and interactivity depending on whether there will be a facilitator present to moderate the process of understanding and learning.

You have four main choices with regard to human support for online learning; you can provide:

- the support mainly face to face

- the support online or by the use of other technology such as phone, email, text or chat

- a combination of online, other technology and face-to-face support

- no human support.

Face-to-face support suits a blended approach to the online element; that is, where there is a relationship between online and face-to-face delivery. When learning providers use online content to enhance traditional live delivery, it is possible to provide the human support for learning face to face. In reality, even tutors who meet their learners regularly may resort to using email, phone calls, texting or chat to keep in touch from time to time.

Face-to-face support enables the facilitator to put a face to a name, establish a working relationship with the learner based on interaction in the real world, and make use of the visual cues absent from interactions mediated by the technology.

If learners live far away from the education and training provider and cannot travel regularly or at all to meet the tutors, if the nature of learners' lives (perhaps they work part time or full time) means they cannot find time to meet up with tutors, or if the course is delivered totally online, the only real option is to offer support online and/or via other technology.

According to research by Kearsley (2000), encouraging a high degree of interactivity and participation is the most important role of a facilitator in an online class. The role of and skills required by individuals who support learners online are covered in Chapter 4: *Delivering learning online*. Consider the timing, amount and methods of support, other than face to face, for learners.

When deciding the timing of the support you will offer learners, remember why your learners cannot meet you face to face. If they work full time during the day, for example, you may need to be available to them in the evenings and at weekends. If they work shifts, you may need to stagger your support across a combination of evenings, day time and weekends.

The level of support must be agreed in advance. Will you be available for two hours one evening a week? Three hours during usual office hours? One hour over a weekend? You must decide when and for how long you will make yourself available to learners, when planning a course.

Finally, you must decide how learners will be able to contact you, and whether this access will be online as part of the course using a combination of asynchronous and synchronous tools, or via other means such as phone. Some facilitators choose a combination of communication methods according to learners and their circumstances.

Whatever decision you make about computer-mediated support, clarity about how and when learners can contact you is essential. There is nothing worse than learners not knowing when the facilitator will participate in an online session, or how to contact the facilitator if there is a problem.

If you decide that the online offer must stand alone and not be facilitated in any way, make sure that the manner in which the materials are presented, any activities and the navigation provided support learners in achieving their learning objectives.

Overall, the level of support you give determines the level of complexity of the content you can use.

## Working through the materials

> *'Tell me and I forget, show me and I remember, involve me and I understand.'*
>
> Chinese proverb

Learning is more likely to be effective if the learner is active rather than passive. Learners must be given opportunities to practise and interact with the materials as well as with facilitators and other learners.

In a traditional classroom environment, the tutor can see instantly when a learner is being left behind, and can help learners or compensate for the shortcomings of any materials by providing additional explanations, guidance and other support.

Online learning materials, however, must stand alone – even within a facilitated course. Materials that are hard to use or difficult to navigate will result in your learners losing interest and motivation.

As you create online materials, put yourself in the place of your intended learners and ask yourself these questions:

- Where am I within the online course or activity?
- What am I supposed to be doing?
- What am I aiming to achieve?
- What am I learning through this activity?
- Where do I go next and how do I get there?

If you know the answers at all stages of working through your content and activities, your learners should not have a problem navigating your online learning environment. If you cannot answer these questions, you will need to review the design of your online learning space and be more explicit in your directions and explanations.

You must decide whether learners work through the materials in a linear fashion – whether they must complete one activity before they can move forward – or whether additional information and signposting is required to enable them to decide what to learn and what sections to complete in what order. If there are assessment activities, make it clear to learners whether these activities are mandatory and how they fit in with the learning materials.

Feedback is an important element in online learning – it provides positive reinforcement for learners, which in turn acts as motivation. Feedback should be targeted, meaningful and relevant, and used to reinforce the teaching point.

When you create your materials, consider how you will provide feedback to your learners. Many learning platforms incorporate methods of giving feedback, but if yours does not, you could use, for example, personal email, a live internet phone conversation, online chat, or maybe a one-to-one or group discussion forum.

You have similar decisions to make about the submission of written assignments and project work. Again, your learning platform may provide facilities to develop such activities, but if it does not, you will need to decide how your learners will send you their work – perhaps by email attachment, an instant message service or by uploading a file to a website via FTP (File Transfer Protocol).

> **Pause and reflect**
>
> The questions to ask at this stage of the design process are:
>
> - How will learners access the learning content and activities? What implications does this have on how you write and present the materials?
>
> - What tools do you have available to develop and amend online content and activities?

## Accessibility

Accessibility is important in the context of technology-assisted delivery of learning, and must be addressed both when designing online activities and creating digital resources. Being able to cater for different needs is not only good practice, but a legal requirement. Most countries now have some form of accessibility legislation.

An effective initial assessment procedure should enable you to identify from the start those learners who need extra support or have specific technical requirements. Also consider people with access to only limited IT equipment, people with slow internet connections, people for whom English is not their native language and individuals who are not confident readers or writers.

Ensure that details of minimum hardware and software requirements are included in your marketing and enrolment materials.

There are number of factors to bear in mind when developing your online space with accessibility in mind, including:

- **Screen design**: Screens should be clear and uncluttered, and each should function in a consistent manner, with navigation controls in the same position on every screen.

Consider that some learners may access parts of your online provision via a mobile phone or other handheld device. Mobile learning (m-learning) is useful as a way of revisiting and revising topics. It is less useful at covering new material for the first time or enabling work online, since screen sizes are so small. Screen size may become less of an issue in the future as handheld technologies develop and improve.

- **Colour**: Use high-contrast colours, such as black text on a light background so that text is clear.

  Do not refer to screen features by colour – for example, 'click on the green button' – because this may confuse colour-blind users or those with visual impairments who see colours differently.

- **Text and graphics**: Use the ALT (alternative) tags facility to provide text descriptions of any images used. The ALT tag should provide a clear, concise description of the essential information conveyed by the image, and there should be a consistent use of descriptive labels on all navigation controls.

- **Navigation**: Some learners do not use a mouse, or may have difficulty using one. Ensure that it is possible to navigate your materials using the keyboard. Learners may use the Tab key to move between active areas of the screen; the way in which a learner tabs through the navigation controls should be consistent on every screen.

- **Multimedia**: Provide a text transcript for all video, animation and audio content for learners with hearing impairments and those who do not have sound cards and/or speakers installed on their computers. Any transcript of a video or animation should include descriptions of what is taking place and not just the words being spoken.

- **Activities**: Some activities, such as drag-and-drop activities, are difficult to make fully accessible. Consider providing an equivalent accessible alternative in these cases.

For more information on all these accessibility issues, see the model for m-learning and accessibility on the TechDis website [http://www.techdis.ac.uk/index.php?p=9_5].

The TechDis website [http://www.techdis.ac.uk/index.php?p=1] has a wealth of information relating to how digital content can be made more accessible. You can also find guidance on the Staff development e-learning centre (SDELC) website [http://www.sdelc.org.uk] – log in and navigate to **Common modules** > **Extended common modules** > **E-learning and accessibility**.

You can find further information about accessibility legislation in Appendix B: 'Accessibility websites'.

> **Pause and reflect**
>
> The question to ask at this stage of the design process is:
>
> - What accessibility issues may your potential learners have when using online facilities and resources and how might you address these issues?

## Checklist: Your learning space

You can use this checklist to help you plan your online learning provision in your own organisation.

|  | Yes | No | Perhaps |
|---|---|---|---|
| **Who am I planning to deliver to – have I identified my learner attributes?** | | | |
| Age range | | | |
| Gender and culture | | | |
| Location | | | |
| Education and work background | | | |
| Abilities | | | |
| Attitudes to learning | | | |
| Pre-existing topic knowledge and understanding | | | |
| Levels of competency in using computer technology and their experiences with online learning | | | |
| Possible constraints | | | |
| **Have I defined my learning outcomes?** | | | |
| **What type of online provision am I aiming to deliver?** | | | |
| Fully-facilitated online courses or opportunities | | | |
| Fully-facilitated blended courses or opportunities | | | |
| Self-directed online courses or opportunities | | | |
| Online learning objects to enhance face-to-face courses or opportunities | | | |
| Online conference or event | | | |

|  | Yes | No | Perhaps |
|---|---|---|---|
| **What learning platform will I use to deliver?** | | | |
| Virtual Learning Environment – commercial | | | |
| Virtual Learning Environment – open source | | | |
| Website/web portal | | | |
| Content Management System (CMS) | | | |
| Intranet | | | |
| Shared folders | | | |
| Storage devices (eg CD-ROM/DVD/USB memory device) | | | |
| A combination of platforms | | | |
| **How will I deliver my learning materials?** | | | |
| Asynchronously | | | |
| Synchronously | | | |
| A mixture of asynchronous and synchronous | | | |
| **What will my content mainly consist of?** | | | |
| Text-based | | | |
| Audio | | | |
| Video | | | |
| Questions | | | |
| Games | | | |
| Simulations | | | |
| Reflection-based | | | |
| Research-based | | | |
| A mixture of text and media | | | |

|  | Yes | No | Perhaps |
|---|---|---|---|
| **What format will my online element take?** | | | |
| Totally online with no face-to-face delivery | | | |
| Part of a face-to-face activity | | | |
| Part of a face-to-face course | | | |
| Supplementary to a face-to-face session | | | |
| **What human support am I going to provide?** | | | |
| Mainly face to face | | | |
| Online or using other technology | | | |
| A combination of face-to-face, online and other technology | | | |
| None | | | |
| **How will my learners work through the materials?** | | | |
| In a linear fashion | | | |
| In a non-linear fashion | | | |
| **How will I provide feedback to my learners on their completed activities?** | | | |
| Via the learning platform feedback tools | | | |
| Via personal email | | | |
| Via telephone | | | |
| Via personal chat or forum | | | |
| Via a face-to-face meeting | | | |
| Via a combination of tools | | | |
| **Are my materials accessible?** | | | |

# Chapter 3
# Developing online provision

If you are developing online learning provision from scratch, you first need to consider your approach to your online development and building a team to implement your approach. The most important aspect to consider is staffing. What model of staffing will your organisation adopt and develop? What impact will there be on staff by developing online learning as part of your provision? How will relevant staff skills be developed? What roles will be created? This chapter considers these points in more detail.

## Organisational models

Your organisation's model for incorporating online learning methodologies into its teaching and learning provision is likely to be influenced by its culture and the resources available. Consider, for example, these questions:

- Is the culture of your organisation open to change, innovation and risk taking?

- What is the motivation for making the shift towards online learning provision?

- Will there be an organisation-wide approach or will it be a more localised approach with only a few staff utilising online delivery and doing so in their own fashion?

- Will there be buy-in from all staff: tutors, support staff and managers?

- Will there be support and financial backing for the training needs of staff and the necessary developmental work?

- Is finance available to buy and maintain a commercial learning platform such as a Virtual Learning Environment (VLE), or will you look at open source VLEs or another form of learning platform?

## Organisation-wide approach

Utilising standard course designs across the curriculum and focusing on the benefits of reusable content, this model is likely to be driven from above and focus on the financial benefits.

The downside to this model is that it adopts a 'one size fits all' approach which may be perceived as inappropriate for delivering flexible online learning.

In addition, staff may feel pressurised into adopting online learning. Without the appropriate training and development, staff may be unlikely to buy in to online learning or maximise its potential.

## Localised approach

This model is likely to be driven by individual online champions within the organisation who are more likely to build their own communities of practice, share experiences, gain a deeper understanding of the processes involved, and enthuse and encourage others within the organisation to engage in online developments.

## The online learning team

### Defining the terminology

As with many areas of education and training, different sectors and organisations sometimes use different terms for job roles.

The same is true when we talk about online learning, particularly the people who deliver the learning. In online learning, a different relationship develops between the learner and the person delivering the learning as the learner becomes more proactive in their learning. This more equitable online relationship has led to some people referring to these online deliverers as online tutors, e-tutors, facilitators, moderators or something completely different.

Many people would say that an online tutor/e-tutor simply delivers learning online, rather than face-to-face. But delivering learning online requires a specific set of skills. It involves the ability to articulate concepts, manage a tutor group, guide people through the learning experience and help them to become more active learners within a predominantly text-based environment. Delivering learning online is about motivating learners and encouraging interaction and communication in an online environment. It is about assessing learners, dealing with any conflicts and difficulties and advising on or solving access or other technical problems. All of these aspects are covered in more detail later in this chapter.

While the terms online tutor and e-tutor are frequently used, they do not necessarily encompass the full role of the learning deliverer. Some argue that the term moderator should be used, but others associate this term with the accreditation process. The term moderator can sound quite controlling and authoritative, whereas the term facilitator suggests being helped and guided, rather than talked down to. Others interpret a moderator as someone who only moderates discussions and does not adopt the wider role of an online learning deliverer.

In this publication – and for the NIACE Online Course Delivery project – we use the term **facilitator** because we feel that this term better encompasses their job.

As we said in Chapter 1: *Learning and the role of online delivery,* online learning has the potential to engage learners who have diverse learning styles. Online learning is learner-centred and encourages active learning and reflection. Online learning encourages a move away from a didactic tutor-led learning style in which the tutor delivers information (the 'sage on the stage') to a more interactive, constructivist style in which the facilitator collaborates in the learning process (the 'guide on the side').

> '*I am looking forward to working with all of you, and during the course I am sure I shall learn a few new things as well as you as I am only a facilitator and not the fount of all knowledge.*'
>
> Quote from an experienced online facilitator for NIACE online course delivery project, in a welcoming discussion forum (2007)

## Building a team

While the facilitator will play a major role in the success of your online delivery, a host of other people also contribute to the creation, running, evaluation and success of your online project. For online learning to succeed, it helps to have a solid team.

Ideally, you should embed online course development into your existing course development structure. You will need someone to take responsibility for the design of the course – preferably someone who has expertise in curriculum design. Likewise, as in all course development, there is a need for a course co-ordinator. However, due to the nature of online delivery, people with other skills sets are required to assist the curriculum specialists.

Many roles need to be filled – some tasks may be shared across different roles, others may be combined and given to one person. Depending on the type of adult learning service you provide, you may already have everyone you need to fulfil the different roles, or initially you may have to work with a limited number of people and learn as you progress. It is always good practice to involve your learners the curriculum design process – at the very least by inviting learners to trial your online learning space and materials. Let us assume that you are starting an online project from scratch and explore what your dream team would look like.

A wide range of tasks must be completed to create and support the delivery of online learning, including:

- design of the online provision

- development of the learning space

- creation of the online learning materials and collaborative activities

- implementation and maintenance of the delivery system (the VLE, intranet or website/web portal)

- research and compilation of other relevant resources such as e-journals, e-books and other web-based resources

- provision of staff development opportunities to ensure that individuals have the skills to deliver learning and support online learners

- organisation and management of the move from traditional face-to-face delivery to blended or online delivery.

If you are approaching these tasks from an organisational perspective, you will need to consider who will carry them out. Let us look first at the option of developing and delivering a fully facilitated online course, because the people involved would be involved whatever your intended online learning provision is. Then we can consider any additional roles that may be needed for other aspects of online delivery such as online conferencing. You may use different team member titles for some of these roles.

| Team role | Responsibilities |
|---|---|
| **Project manager/ team leader** | To oversee the entire project; hold your organisation's present and future vision; lead, inspire and enthuse; control budgets; generally develop the project team; and communicate to the project team (and beyond) and make things happen. To identify and recruit other project staff. And to agree a structure to the course or event with the course co-ordinator and any relevant facilitators to achieve the intended learning outcomes. |
| **Course co-ordinator** | To ensure the course area is correctly developed, oversee the delivery of the course, and act as a first point of contact for the facilitators. To undertake a final evaluation of the course, finalise the quality control process and produce end-of-course reports. |
| **Administrator** | To support the team from concept to delivery. To arrange any face-to-face venues, couriers or accommodation required – if your course is blended, for example – or to cover the administrative aspects associated with online delivery. |
| **Technical support** | To ensure that the delivery platform is well maintained and robust; to provide advice, guidance and support to your facilitators, learners and other project team members; and to provide asset management. |
| **Content author(s)/editor(s)** | To create your materials from scratch, amend existing digital content, or convert existing face-to-face materials to a format suitable for online delivery. Also to create the supporting documentation for the course: handbooks, how–tos, learner agreements, certificates and so forth. |

| Team role | Responsibilities |
|---|---|
| **Course technical designer(s)** | To undertake any technical conversion work necessary to make your materials fully accessible and ensure they work on your learning platform. To create any multimedia content required. |
| **Marketing officer** | To research your target audience, market and advertise your courses, and set up your enrolment system. |
| **Admissions/enrolment officer** | To oversee enrolment and deal with any issues involved. |
| **Facilitator(s)** | To deliver the course. Ideally your facilitator(s) will have the relevant subject knowledge and the ability to offer individual tutor support in an online environment. |
| **Assessors** | To assess learners' portfolios if you are offering an accredited course. |
| **Moderators** (internal and external) | To oversee the accreditation process if you are offering an accredited course. |
| **Accreditation officer/ administrator** | To deal with the administration associated with the moderation requirements. |
| **Finance officer** | To oversee the budget and deal with income generated if you are charging learners for the course. |
| **Learners** | To trial and evaluate the online learning space and resources. In some cases to contribute to the content. |
| **Other** | If you are producing video, audio or animation materials or online materials for distribution on CD-ROM or DVD, you may also need the services of a multimedia expert, a printer and a media replicator. |
| | If you are running online conferences, you may need to provide additional support to your online speakers in using your chosen delivery technology and in creating their resources. |

**Table 2:** *The ideal dream team*

So this is the dream team. But what if you do not have a full project team behind you? You could combine many of the roles above. For example, one person could carry out all the administration tasks and also be responsible for producing some of the supporting documentation. The facilitators may be involved in creating the course content, and the technical staff may play a role in converting the materials for delivery on your chosen delivery platform. Your organisation may need to start small and pick and mix the roles listed above to meet the needs of your learners. This is particularly true if you adopt a localised rather than an organisation-wide approach to incorporating online learning methodologies into your organisation's teaching and learning provision.

Once the course has been developed, subsequent delivery costs and time are reduced – especially if your project team is not changing too much. This is one of the advantages to having your materials in an online format: you can review and amend at a much lower cost than if all your materials are hard copies.

NIACE's experience shows that to create from scratch a text-based ten-week, level-3-accredited online course for up to 20 learners and involving two facilitators, took about 64 days in total. This total covers the course development from conception to point of delivery. Subsequent deliveries of the course take about 50 days from the point at which the content has been created. This total includes the facilitators', team leader's, administrator's and technical time. (See Appendix C: 'Example of time taken by NIACE for initial course creation and delivery' for more details).

As with any new project, having the right staff in the right roles is crucial. For your online learning provision to succeed, you may need to develop the skills of some of your staff, in particular those of the online facilitator. Chapter 4: *Delivering learning online* looks at the various skills sets and roles required in more detail.

> **Pause and reflect**
>
> Consider your own organisation and the people within it:
>
> - What approach will you take to incorporate online learning in your teaching and learning provision? Do you already have people to join your online provision project team?
>
> - Do you have the necessary funding and infrastructure in place already, or do you need to address these first?

## Setting up your course

Once you are ready to set up your course, you need to consider what you should include in your course area. NIACE's experience suggests that you include the following:

- An overview of the course

- The aims, objectives and learning outcomes for the whole course and for each of its sections (each unit, module, session, and chunk of learning)

- Tracking documentation to help learners meet the course requirements (see Appendix D: 'Example assessment and tracking sheet for learners' for examples from a NIACE online course)

- A list of all learners on the course and the names of any facilitators

- A course schedule or calendar

- The learning content and activities, including a content outline that describes the materials and the sequence in which they will appear. Use a standard, consistent approach to signposting within the area – such as module and section headings, breadcrumb trials, numbering sequences and activity icons

- A social online area for informal discussions

- A help and advice area that could include a frequently asked questions (FAQ) section. Ensure that you set out the ground rules here and provide guidelines on how to use any tools you will provide during the course. You should also include an electronic version of the learner handbook and of any how-to guides, information about how and when to contact the facilitator(s) and details of any technical support available. You should also set up a support area for facilitators

- An acceptable use policy (see Appendix E: 'Acceptable use policy for the NIACE Moodle' for an example).

## The importance of including a social area

A social and general interest area is the first item you should strongly consider creating within your course area. Within a traditional face-to-face learning environment, as the weeks progress, learners in a class interact with each other (and the tutor) socially. This may be just a quick chat before or after the class or during a coffee break, or it may even progress to trips to the nearest pub after the class, or indeed social meetings outside class. Many lasting friendships have been forged through adult learning classes. A social area within your online course will enable a similar – albeit virtual – social interaction to take place between your learners.

The NIACE online course areas, for example, always include a NIACE Village Pub and Restaurant discussion forum, which is open and promoted during the induction session. Indeed, the first activity that NIACE participants embark on is to enter the forum and post introductory messages about themselves as part of an ice-breaker activity. Some NIACE facilitators encourage the continued use of the social forum by nominating a different learner each week to host a themed virtual party.

Another reason for including a social area is that even though the majority of learners now have broadband internet access, there are still people who are restricted to dial-up access using a 56k modem. For these people, every minute online must be cost effective and purposeful. If your course discussion forums fill up with general chit-chat, these users may become disillusioned and frustrated at wasting time online looking for relevant postings about the course topics. By keeping the social interactions in one place, you allow these learners to choose whether to spend their online time socially interacting or concentrating on their learning.

While ideally you will encourage all of your learners to participate in the social interaction elements of your course, it should not be made mandatory, and you must accept that some learners (just as in a traditional face-to-face setting) will choose not to engage in social networking, even if they are not restricted by costly access to the internet or other commitments on their time.

## Layout and release of learning materials

Decide how and when to release learning materials to your learners. Your choices depend upon the way you run your course and, to a greater extent, whether you include collaborative group activities.

If you release all the learning materials on day 1, some of your learners may try to complete the entire course as quickly as possible. If you want learners to do this, and the materials are predominantly designed for self-study and little interaction, this is not an issue. However, if your intention is to guide learners through the materials as a group and for them to engage in collaborative group activities or participate in group discussions, there will be issues if some of your learners have raced ahead. Not only with the forerunners have no-one to collaborate with, but those bringing up the rear will find it difficult to contribute if the forerunners have already done all the work or made all the valid discussion points.

If you choose not to release all the materials on day 1, it is, however, important that you give your participants an insight into what content is to come and when.

You may wish to incorporate some catch-up time. All learners have different speeds of working, especially adult learners with other work and life commitments. It is good practice to consider including some extra time in your course to enable learners to catch up. NIACE online courses, as a rule, extend course delivery time by two weeks so that, for example, a notional ten-week online course is delivered over 12 weeks to allow for different engagement and learning times.

## Incorporating computer-mediated communication tools within your course

When designing and creating your online learning content, you should incorporate some computer-mediated communication (CMC) opportunities to enable your learners to work together and participate in group activities.

CMC tools are a popular component in online learning. They can enhance courses in a variety of ways, by, for example:

- extending time for discussion following an activity to allow for reflection and further comment

- requiring learners to move beyond simply reading and accepting supplied material, by engaging them in critical debate on the topic

- providing an outlet for learners to pose questions and receive feedback, not only from the facilitator but also from their peers

- allowing learners to share information or references with each other, for example book reviews or recommended websites.

There are also suggestions that electronic collaboration offers significant benefits for learning:

- Online collaborative tools and processes focus on content rather than personalities, and actively encourage participation.

- The focus on writing skills can encourage thinking skills – writing is usually (but not always) more precise than speech, and online contribution offers learners the opportunity to reflect and clarify thoughts before sharing them.

- There is evidence to indicate that writing is linked to higher-order thinking (including the ability to analyse, interpret, evaluate and respond); online communication has potential to improve learners' critical thought processes.

- On a pragmatic level, collaborative tools encourage peer-to-peer activity. Learning from each other can be a powerful experience.

However, there are some issues to consider when using CMC on your course. In particular, the characteristics of individual learners may affect the way you use a collaborative approach:

- The lack of visual or verbal clues can sometimes lead to misinterpretation. This may make some learners reluctant to contribute.

- Some learners will expect instant responses and/or solutions, which may lead to issues either being resolved too quickly or not quickly enough.

- Learners with poor typing skills may feel at a disadvantage.

- Learners working in a second language may feel reluctant to contribute.

As well as CMC tools, you may want to incorporate other tools in your online learning provision. When deciding which CMC tools to use within your course, remember that most technology tools can be viewed as enabling either asynchronous or synchronous activity. Most of the tools listed below are available if you have access to a Virtual Learning Environment (VLE), but if you are not using a VLE, you should be able to find internet-based solutions to tie in with your learning materials. Asynchronous and synchronous tools, and VLEs were covered in more detail in Chapter 2: 'Designing the learning space'.

## Overview of computer-mediated communication tools and other technologies

### Discussion forum

**Definition**: An online community where participants may read and post topics of common interest or discuss course-related topics asynchronously.

Discussion forums are one way of enabling learners to work together as a group. Discussion forums generally appear in a threaded (topic-related) format. Within a discussion, learners can debate several topics simultaneously. Learners can choose how messages are displayed on their computers: by topic (the replies to an initial post are indented under the initial post) or in chronological order of posting.

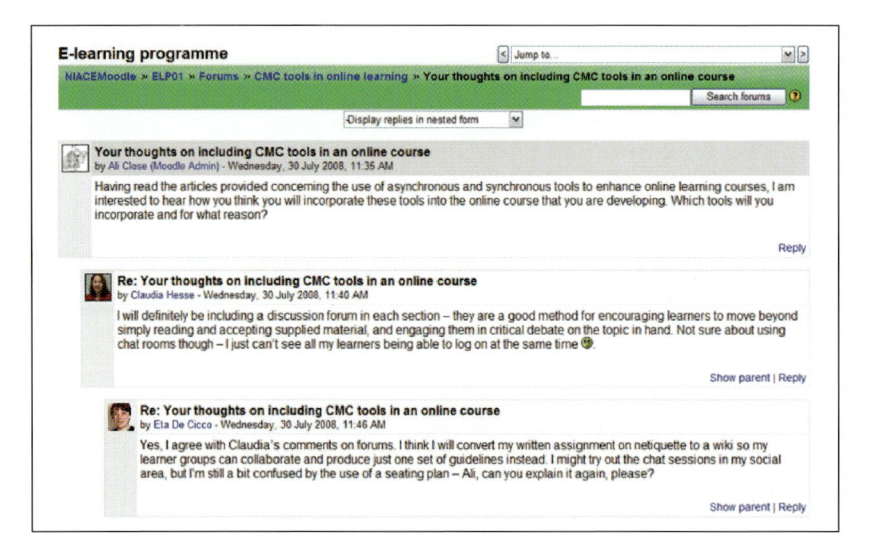

**Figure 3:** *Example of a threaded discussion forum*

Facilitators can move posts to the correct forums if learners accidently post to the wrong place. Facilitators can also remove inappropriate or offensive posts.

Most discussion forums allow you to select an option that result in copies of the messages being sent to your email address (as well as remaining within the discussion forum). This can be very beneficial for facilitators, who can easily gain an overview of learners' participation in different forums without having to go to the VLE, intranet or a website/web portal where the individual groups are located.

Discussion forums can be referred back to during a course. However, some learners may feel uneasy about their comments being there for all to see. Also, some learners, if they are never online at the same time as their peers, may find that this form of communication heightens feelings of learning in isolation.

Discussion groups are hugely popular on the internet. If you are not using a VLE, there are both commercial and freeware discussion forum systems available.

## Wikis

> **Definition**: Areas designed to enable learners and facilitators to contribute to or modify the content. Wikipedia [http://en.wikipedia.org] is one of the best known wikis. Wiki is originally a Hawaiian word meaning fast.

A wiki works on the same principle as a discussion forum: it encourages learners to collaborate and share their views. However, whereas a discussion forum is linear in appearance, a wiki enables learners to share ideas in much the same way as you might capture points from a discussion on an electronic whiteboard or a flipchart. A wiki has the added benefit that you can edit other people's contributions and track changes by date and the individual who made them.

Wikis can be used within an online course to encourage learners to develop group ideas for a project or to produce a collaborative resource as part of an activity or assignment. The facility to track changes is useful for formative assessment, when a facilitator might want to see how an assignment has evolved and who has contributed to it.

Numerous commercial and freeware wikis are available on the internet. As with all web-based solutions, you need to find a wiki that can be made private and accessible only to your learners – not only to provide them with a safe learning environment, but also because of the risk of spam or hacking attacks.

## Chat rooms

> **Definition**: Areas in which learners with a common interest can communicate in real time.

Chat sessions can help learners feel part of the learning community and alleviate feelings of learning in isolation.

However, using chat rooms within an online learning course does require planning, because of their synchronous nature. You will need to advertise the chat to ensure that your learners can all be online at the given time. You may need to offer several options to account for your learners' other commitments and online attendance patterns.

Chat rooms are not without their disadvantages. People who can type fast may dominate the conversation, and because of the real-time nature of the conversation (ie it appears on screen as it is typed rather than in a threaded format), the conversation can quickly become bewildering and nonsensical.

Many web-based chat rooms are available. More tips on running a successful chat session are provided in Appendix F: 'Guidelines for facilitating online chat sessions'.

## Instant messaging

> **Definition**: A rapid means of communicating online. Learners know when others are online and can have a real-time conversation in a private chat room.

Facilitators can use instant messaging to send a message to one or several participants, and learners can use instant messaging to send private messages to their peers or facilitator(s).

While you may not want to use instant messaging for collaborative activities, it is a useful tool for building a sense of community and providing learners with instant feedback. Instant messaging can help alleviate feelings of learning in isolation.

Most VLEs and web-based solutions allow individuals to show when they are online, therefore learners can instantly see if their peers or facilitators are available and communicate with them in a secure and private setting.

## Blogs

> **Definition**: Online diaries, maintained on a regular basis with articles published in reverse chronological order. Blogs represent the personal views of the author.

Blogs are a type of online diary and can be used within online courses for reflective activities, either personally or collaboratively. Many blogs within a VLE or web-based environment enable users to comment on the author's entries.

Learners can use blogs to create personal accounts of their progress on a course or during an event. Web-based solutions enable learners to make their blogs public or keep them private, but be aware that in some VLEs, the blog settings are such that the blog will be visible to any registered user, whether on the same course or not.

Some VLEs incorporate a journal facility that works on the same principle as a blog, but is visible only to learners and their facilitator(s). The facilitator can provide feedback on entries. If your course is based on the principle of the learner as a reflective practitioner, or if your course is designed to help participants meet their continuing professional development (CPD) needs, this facility has enormous benefit.

## Tools specific to a virtual learning environment

The tools mentioned above are all quite common in online learning, and are usually provided within a VLE. In addition, your chosen VLE may have other facilities that can support and enhance the learner experience, such as quiz creation tools, workshop spaces, databases, and feedback and survey tools. You may be able to buy in or acquire additional functionality such as e-assessment tools and file storage and file sharing facilities. It is worth familiarising yourself with your chosen VLE before you finalise your course materials, so that you can take advantage of the numerous learning enhancement tools available.

## Other tools

If you are not using a VLE, but have some ideas on how you would like to incorporate a collaborative activity, a search on the internet may provide a solution for you.

Depending on the topic of your course, you may want to maximise the benefits of using an online environment for delivery and address the needs of different learning styles by including more media-rich content such as images, video, audio and animation. This will require additional hardware and software, and possibly further skills development, depending on who will produce the content. See Chapter 5: 'Sourcing and creating content' for more information on content creation, and Chapter 4: 'Delivering learning online' for more on the skills required.

## A final word on computer-mediated communication tools

Computer-mediated communication activities can enhance your learning materials and make the content more interesting and relevant to participants. Learners can draw upon and share their experiences.

There is no limit to how many CMC activities you include in your online course, but you should bear in mind your target audience, their likely online learning patterns and the relevance of collaborative activities to the overall aims and learning outcomes. If you have many collaborative activities, your learners will often need to be online together. Too many discussion forums, if they are a mandatory part of the course, can be off-putting to learners. Just because you can include a collaborative activity, does not mean that you should include a collaborative activity. Before including it, consider – does this add value to the learning, or will it frustrate and stress my learners?

> **Pause and reflect**
>
> Look back at a learning event in which you were a participant and which you rated as effective and successful.
>
> - What features of the event worked for you?
>
> - Which of these features you would want to replicate in an online environment and why?

## Checklist:
## Your online provision development

You can use these checklists to help you plan your online learning provision in your own organisation.

| | Yes | No | Perhaps |
|---|---|---|---|
| **What is my approach to online development?** | | | |
| Forms part of an organisation wide strategy | | | |
| A localised approach | | | |

| | Want | Already have | Need to appoint/ go external |
|---|---|---|---|
| **What roles are necessary to deliver the online provision? Does my organisation have individuals with these skills already or will I need to appoint or go to an external provider?** | | | |
| **Fully-facilitated online courses** | | | |
| Project manager/team leader | | | |
| Course co-ordinator | | | |
| Administrator | | | |
| Technical support | | | |
| Content author(s)/editor(s) | | | |
| Course technical designer(s) | | | |
| Marketing officer | | | |
| Admissions/enrolment officer | | | |
| Facilitators | | | |
| Assessors | | | |
| Moderators (internal) | | | |
| Moderators (external) | | | |
| Accreditation officer/administrator | | | |

|  | Want | Already have | Need to appoint/ go external |
|---|---|---|---|
| Finance officer |  |  |  |
| Multimedia expert |  |  |  |
| Media replicator |  |  |  |
| **Fully-facilitated blended courses** |  |  |  |
| Project manager/team leader |  |  |  |
| Course co-ordinator |  |  |  |
| Administrator |  |  |  |
| Technical support |  |  |  |
| Content author(s)/editor(s) |  |  |  |
| Course technical designer(s) |  |  |  |
| Marketing officer |  |  |  |
| Admissions/enrolment officer |  |  |  |
| Venue staff (and couriers) |  |  |  |
| Facilitators |  |  |  |
| Assessors |  |  |  |
| Moderators (internal) |  |  |  |
| Moderators (external) |  |  |  |
| Accreditation officer/administrator |  |  |  |
| Finance officer |  |  |  |
| Multimedia expert |  |  |  |
| Media replicator |  |  |  |
| **Self-directed online courses** |  |  |  |
| Project manager/team leader |  |  |  |
| Course co-ordinator |  |  |  |
| Administrator |  |  |  |
| Technical support |  |  |  |
| Content author(s)/editor(s) |  |  |  |
| Course technical designer(s) |  |  |  |

## 72 Developing online provision

|  | Want | Already have | Need to appoint/ go external |
|---|---|---|---|
| Marketing officer |  |  |  |
| Admissions/enrolment officer |  |  |  |
| Finance officer |  |  |  |
| Multimedia expert |  |  |  |
| Media replicator |  |  |  |
| **Online learning objects to enhance face-to-face courses** | | | |
| Project manager/team leader |  |  |  |
| Course co-ordinator |  |  |  |
| Administrator |  |  |  |
| Technical support |  |  |  |
| Content author(s)/editor(s) |  |  |  |
| Course technical designer(s) |  |  |  |
| Multimedia expert |  |  |  |
| Media replicator |  |  |  |
| **Online conferences or events** | | | |
| Project manager/team leader |  |  |  |
| Course co-ordinator |  |  |  |
| Administrator |  |  |  |
| Technical support |  |  |  |
| Content author(s)/editor(s) |  |  |  |
| Course technical designer(s) |  |  |  |
| Marketing officer |  |  |  |
| Admissions/enrolment officer |  |  |  |
| Facilitators |  |  |  |
| Moderators (internal) |  |  |  |
| Moderators (external) |  |  |  |
| Finance officer |  |  |  |
| Multimedia expert |  |  |  |
| Media replicator |  |  |  |
| Guest speakers |  |  |  |
| Additional support for speakers |  |  |  |

| What will my course area look like? | | | |
|---|---|---|---|
| | Yes | No | Perhaps |
| **What will I include in my course area?** | | | |
| Overview of the course | | | |
| Aims, objectives and learning outcomes (for whole course) | | | |
| Aims, objectives and learning outcomes (for each section, lesson, module etc) | | | |
| Tracking documentation | | | |
| List of all participants | | | |
| Course schedule/calendar | | | |
| Learning content and activities | | | |
| Social area | | | |
| FAQ/help and advice area | | | |
| Course and CMC ground rules | | | |
| Electronic handbook/how to guides | | | |
| Standard consistent signposting | | | |
| Acceptable use policy for learning platform | | | |
| **How will I release my materials online?** | | | |
| All at once when the course begins | | | |
| At regular intervals during the course | | | |
| **What CMC tools will I incorporate?** | | | |
| Discussion forum | | | |
| Wikis | | | |
| Chat rooms | | | |
| Instant messaging | | | |
| Blogs | | | |
| Reflective journals | | | |
| VLE specific tools | | | |

# Chapter 4:
# Delivering learning online

Chapter 3: 'Developing online provision' looked at the factors involved in developing online programmes and activities, including building up your team and setting up your course area. In this chapter, we look at the actual delivery of an online course.

It is impossible to explore delivering online events and programmes without first considering staff skills. Learning providers need to ensure that members of staff have the additional skills to manage and teach effectively within an online environment. Learners, too, need guidance on what to expect and what is acceptable behaviour within an online environment, and they may need support to develop additional skills to successfully engage with the course and achieve their maximum potential.

Let us look first at the skills required across the whole organisation to incorporate online delivery, and then explore the specific skills required by an online facilitator. Chapter 3: 'Developing online provision' identified the roles required for online delivery. In Table 3 below, we revisit these roles and look at their associated skills. There may be some overlap between the skills sets required across the various roles.

| Role | People/team | Skills required | Additional skills |
|---|---|---|---|
| Team leader | Project manager/team leader | Project management.<br><br>The ability to enthuse and encourage staff new to online learning provision. | |
| Technical support | IT technicians<br>Web developers<br>VLE developers<br>Help desk staff | Maintain and support the IT systems in place for online delivery: web servers, VLE, intranet, website, etc.<br><br>Provide support to all users of the IT systems. | |
| Course development<br><br>Designing and developing the learning space | Content author(s)<br><br>Course designer(s)<br><br>Learning technologists<br><br>To some extent:<br>Course co-ordinator/project officer<br><br>Facilitators<br><br>Editor | Be able to use the software tools for developing materials.<br><br>Understand the pedagogical approach being undertaken – such as self-paced learning or collaborative learning – and ensure the necessary activities can be incorporated to meet the learning objectives in an online environment.<br><br>Know what other electronic resources can be incorporated into the materials or environment.<br><br>Solid understanding of the delivery environment. | |
| Course delivery | Facilitators<br><br>Learning technologists<br><br>To some extent:<br>Course co-ordinator/project officer | Online facilitation.<br><br>Solid understanding of the delivery environment.<br><br>Know the requirements for evaluation and accreditation.<br><br>Have some technical knowledge to support learners, or know who to approach for support. | |

| Role | People/team | Skills required | Additional skills |
|---|---|---|---|
| Support services | Administrator<br><br>Admissions/ enrolment officer<br><br>Assessors<br><br>Moderators<br><br>Accreditation officer/ administrator<br><br>To some extent: Finance officer | Understand the delivery platform being used and organisational processes for marketing, enrolment, finance and accreditation. | Ability to work as part of a team. Ability to project-manage (for some). |

**Table 3:** *Roles and the skills sets required for organisation-wide online delivery*

Depending on whether you take an organisation-wide or localised approach to incorporating online learning provision, there will be some overlap of the roles and skills sets involved. If the approach is localised, in particular, members of staff may well adopt the role of course developer and deliverer, incorporating technical and pedagogical aspects, perhaps because there is no support available within their organisations or because they have developed these skills sets and want to be fully involved in what they are creating and delivering.

## The effective online facilitator

By far, the role that will have the most impact on the success of your online provision is the facilitator. (Of course, if your online provision is purely self-directed study, this role is superfluous. Your learning directives will be the key element to the success of the course.)

Although facilitating online is different to traditional face-to-face teaching, there are many similarities, and some skills are transferable. As with traditional teaching, the methods employed vary depending on the type of course, the subject matter and the participants' individual needs. The main differences between traditional teaching and online facilitation are the:

- lack of body language and vocal clues
- different nature of interaction with the participants
- need for effective time management and flexibility for accessing the course and supporting the participants
- need to develop an online communication style
- use of text as the main type of communication
- constraints of the technology employed.

The facilitator must manage a group of participants, guide them through and assess their learning, interact with them and provide motivation and technical support, and deal with any conflicts or non-participation. In online learning, the role of the facilitator will change as the course progresses. Hislop (2000) lists the following as desirable attributes for online facilitators.

### Attributes of an online facilitator

- **Motivated**: Motivated facilitators have a strong interest in working to make their online courses successful. They are willing to make the effort to deal with technology and a new teaching and learning environment.

- **Approachable**: Approachable facilitators encourage students to interact with them. Being approachable reduces barriers to interaction in the online environment.

- **Visible**: Visible facilitators make their presence felt frequently in the online environment. This helps add substance to the online experience and provide glue to hold the community of learners together.

- **Explicit:** Explicit facilitators provide timely, detailed directions about what learners need to do and how the session will operate. They are also explicit in addressing course content.

- **Pro-active:** Proactive facilitators make an extra effort to reach out to students in ways beyond what would be necessary or typical in a traditional environment. For example, a proactive facilitator might put extra effort into contacting an inactive learner in an online class.

- **Discrete:** Discrete facilitators manage a class without dominating it. They facilitate online discussions while encouraging students to provide most of the comments. They also know when to comment publicly and when to switch to private communication with a learner or learners.

- **Collaborative:** Collaborative facilitators are willing to work with staff and other instructors engaged in online education. They are also comfortable working with learners in a coaching role rather than a more hierarchical style.

- **Technically capable:** Technically capable facilitators have sufficient technical knowledge and skill to be comfortable with the online environment. Online facilitators do not need to be technical experts, but they need basic technical skills to get started. They also need to be able to deal with the inevitable technical glitches and technology changes (with technical support help).

These characteristics focus on how an online facilitator interacts with participants and sets the tone for the tutor group. The role the facilitator adopts should change:

- during the course as the participants become more familiar with the environment and the concept of being an online learner

- in response to the needs and expectations of the participants

- depending on the pedagogical model in use.

As well as displaying Hislop's desirable attributes, an online facilitator may:

- **Convey a sense of belonging**: It is important for the facilitator to convey to all participants that they are part of a course and the wider organisation, and publicise available resources, if appropriate. For example, if your online course is in addition to other traditional courses, participants need to know that they are entitled to a wider range of learner support services offered by the organisation, and how to access them.

- **Set expectations**: The facilitator should ensure that participants know what to expect – and what is expected from them – from the onset of the course. The facilitator should outline participation requirements and ground rules including:

    o how often participants are expected to log on to the course area

    o how to contact the facilitator for support through the forum and by email and phone (and acceptable times to call)

    o how much time participants should spend on activities – including the length of acceptable forum postings and assignment papers

    o acceptable online behaviour when using the online collaboration tools – for example, the use of acceptable language and respect for other participants' views

    o the requirement and method by which participants will

notify the facilitator and other group members of any absence due to holidays or illness

o the timescales within which the facilitator will respond to queries and provide feedback on submitted assignments – if learners know the timeframe within which facilitators will reply, they should not become demotivated by a lack of an instant response. For example, the facilitator may reply to email messages within 48 hours and provide feedback on activities within ten days.

- **Manage the workload**: It is vital that the facilitator decides how much time to spend on the online course. It is very easy, especially in the early days of a course, to spend a great deal of time online and to respond to participants instantly. But this is not a sustainable model – it is not possible or acceptable for the facilitator to work 24 hours a day, 7 days a week, and if participants receive instant responses from the onset of the course, they will continue to expect instant responses. Strategies the facilitator can employ include:

  o Set a personal online schedule – for example, log on to the course for an agreed number of hours every two days, or be online only on certain days of the week. Because of the nature of online learning – any time, any place – the facilitator should aim to be available to participants at different times, including in the evenings and at weekends, where appropriate. If the facilitator has set appropriate ground rules concerning availability to participants, there should not be any problems.

  o Provide a 'help needed' or 'frequently asked questions' discussion forum, where participants are encouraged not only to ask questions, but to offer solutions and advice. The facilitator should not always be the first person to respond – by stepping back and seeing whether other participants respond first, informal group bonding and a sense of community are encouraged.

- **Provide technical support**: Technical support is essential to the success of an online course, but not all facilitators need to be IT experts. The majority of issues experienced by participants are due to lack of confidence in the early parts of the course: not knowing which buttons to press or how to navigate the course area or save documents to their own computers. Before the start of the online course delivery, arrange adequate technical support from the organisation for the facilitator for any unexpected technical problems.

- **Develop an online voice**: When communication is mainly text based, the facilitator needs to develop a style of writing that is appropriate to the learners and the environment. This style should remain friendly and supportive in general, but the facilitator may at times need to sound assertive. Facilitators should be aware of learners' language skills and levels, and adapt their writing to suit. The addition of audio and video communications can enrich communications online, and as the quality of audio and video technology improves, it should become even easier to mix text-based communication with audio and video.

- **Develop skills in managing online communications**: Particularly in the early stages of the course, the facilitator may need to manage discussion forums and chat room sessions effectively. More information about using and managing computer-mediated communication (CMC) tools is covered in Chapter 3: 'Developing online provision'.

- **Conduct one-to-one tutorials using a variety of electronic media**: One-to-one tutorials can be conducted in a variety of ways within an online environment, including through a private chat room session, an instant messaging facility, email or the phone. The facilitator may need to use some or all of these techniques, depending on the individual learners. Some form of record keeping will also need to be developed. See Appendix G: *Contact record sheet* for an example.

- **Provide feedback**: The facilitator can provide feedback to learners in a variety of ways. If you use a Virtual Learning Environment (VLE), there may be facilities built in to enable facilitators to provide feedback for individual activities or assignments. Alternatively, the facilitator may need to use similar methods to those adopted for conducting one-to-one tutorials, in which case some form of record keeping may also need to be developed.

- **Set the right pace**: The facilitator needs to ensure that learners are not bored or struggling to keep up with the course. There may also be issues around learners' preferred learning styles and the suitability of the materials. Regular communication and reflective feedback sessions can address such issues.

- **Develop group and community dynamics/bonding**: As with a traditional face-to-face course, facilitators must understand group dynamics and their impact on collaborative activities.

As in all forms of teaching and learning, the facilitator may need to address additional issues. All learners are different and bring their own personalities, life experiences and expectations to the online environment, as they would to the traditional classroom environment. Additional issues that an online facilitator may face include:

- **Participants who log on to the course or event but do not contribute to activities or group discussions (known as lurkers)**: Some learners may simply need extra encouragement to participate, and the facilitator will need to develop techniques to encourage them. Facilitators must try to find motivational strategies to get learners interested and identify opportunities for individual discussion or collaboration with other learners and/or the facilitator. Facilitators need to consider why learners are lurking – is it because they lack confidence in the subject or their own IT skills? What effect does their lack of contribution have on other participants? But remember, just because someone does not participate in a collaborative activity does not mean they are not actively learning.

- **Participants who have problems accessing the course due to technology issues or lack of computer experience and/or skills**: As discussed above, the facilitator, particularly in the early days of the online course, may need to provide additional technical support or refer the learner to the organisation's IT support facilities. A frequently asked questions area within your course area can provide help and advice about any commonly recurring issues.

- **Individuals working in an environment with few visual clues**: In a mainly text-based environment, if a participant makes an ambiguous posting, it can be difficult to tell whether the message was sarcastic, angry or humorous. Encouraging all participants to use the commonly adopted emoticons (written symbols that denote a mood or expression) can help communication. You can see examples of emoticons in Appendix E: 'Acceptable use policy for the NIACE Moodle'.

- **Individuals who dominate activities and/or discussions, have dominant personalities or flame (display abusive behaviour in collaborative work or discussions)**: Setting ground rules for the use of CMC tools should help. The ground rules could include advice about the length and/or number of contributions, and acceptable tone and language (no swearing, for example).

- **Participants with other pressures and time commitments that impinge on engagement**: If a participant fits the course around other commitments, and is online only when no-one else is, he or she may feel isolated or not have enough self-motivation to maintain engagement in learning. The facilitator needs to intervene and use both asynchronous and synchronous tools to communicate privately with the participant and provide motivation and encouragement.

For further information about the role of the online facilitator, see Berg (1995).

## The successful online learner

To become successful online learners, individuals may need to develop additional skills to those of the traditional classroom-based learner.

Learners who lack computer skills and are unwilling to learn the basics of working online, or who lack self-discipline or self-motivation, tend to be unsuccessful online learners. If online learning needs to be fitted around other commitments, learners should set aside appropriate study time to stay on track and not fall behind.

Learners do not necessarily need to be competent IT users to take part in online learning activities – they will develop IT skills as they participate. However, they will need some initial skills such as being able to use web-based applications and email. Depending on your online provision, learners may also need basic word-processing ability or a familiarity with other software packages. The online learner needs to know these requirements before enrolling and embarking on the online learning journey.

In a facilitated online or blended course, technical support will be available to learners via the facilitator and/or the organisation's IT support provision, and also from their peers and any online technical advice area that the facilitator or course co-ordinator has created.

One benefit of learning online is its flexibility: learners and facilitators do not need to be in a particular place at a set time every week. However, learners do need a disciplined approach to time management, because it is easy to fall behind and be unable to catch up. Learners should be encouraged to access the course at regular intervals to keep up to date, particularly if you use CMC tools and group activities within the learning materials. Learners may spend more time online during the first few weeks of a course while they familiarise themselves with the environment, but, as the course progresses, they may need less time online to keep up to date.

Some learners may need to be encouraged to participate in online discussions. If learners come late to a forum and everything has been said, they may simply put 'I agree' all the time. Some learners may be wary of contributing to a discussion because of the permanent nature of the forum: once posted, their views and comments are there for all to see. If learners are sensitive or worried about being ridiculed by their peers, they may need added encouragement from the facilitator to participate.

All learners are different (as discussed in Chapter 1: 'Learning and the role of online delivery'). While some educationalists may like to pigeon-hole learners into prescribed learning styles, it is important to remember that learners are individuals: some may struggle in an online learning environment while others flourish. It is important to recognise the individual skills, experience and subject knowledge that learners bring to the online environment.

Some learners may expect an online course to be very similar to the traditional classroom setting – the concept of being more involved in the learning process, and the different relationship they will build with their peers and the facilitator, may be alien to them. Learners may need extra guidance at the beginning of the course to help them feel comfortable with having more control over their learning. Learners may also have reservations about the changing relationship with their facilitator as the course progresses. However, for many learners, online learning may prove an ideal alternative and help them succeed when they have failed before in a more traditional learning environment.

**Pause and reflect**

- In what ways do you think that facilitating online differs from facilitating in face-to-face situations?

- What benefits do you think are associated with providing online support?

# Checklist: Your delivery of online learning

You can use this checklist to help you plan your online learning provision in your own organisation.

|  | Yes | No | Perhaps |
|---|---|---|---|
| **How will I develop my staff?** | | | |
| Send them on external courses | | | |
| Develop an in-house training programme | | | |
| Purchase an off-the-shelf training programme | | | |
| Give them control of their own development | | | |
| **Do I have relevant support systems in place?** | | | |
| Technical support for facilitators | | | |
| Technical support for learners | | | |
| Guidelines for facilitators including: | | | |
|     Schemes of work | | | |
|     Welcoming the participants | | | |
|     Supporting the participants | | | |
|     Making materials available | | | |
|     Response times for queries and assignments | | | |
|     Providing feedback | | | |
|     Motivating participants | | | |
|     Dealing with lurkers and non-participants | | | |
|     Record keeping | | | |
|     Monitoring discussion forums | | | |
|     Facilitating chat sessions | | | |
|     Accreditation and e-portfolio requirements | | | |
|     Ending the course | | | |
|     Dealing with withdrawals | | | |

|  | Yes | No | Perhaps |
|---|---|---|---|
| **What other documentation do I need to ensure a consistent approach to my online provision?** | | | |
| Marketing and enrolment information | | | |
| Pre-course information | | | |
| Welcoming emails | | | |
| Induction session guidance | | | |
| Learner agreements | | | |
| Course completion certificates | | | |

# Chapter 5: Sourcing and creating content

## Before you start developing your learning content

The MERLOT Teacher Education programme [http://teachereducation.merlot.org] defines learning material as:

> 'Any digital entity designed to meet a specific learning outcome that can be reused to support learning.'

If we take this definition as a basis, material placed on the internet, an intranet, a learning platform or a website is not strictly learning content if it does not meet one or more learning outcome.

Any digital resource that can be used to support learning is known as a learning object. Learning objects include anything from an image to a combination of different elements – for example, text, audio, video and animation – that together deliver one or more learning outcome. The smallness of each component part, and the number of these parts that can be joined together into a larger whole, determines what is referred to as granularity. Learning objects are especially useful for introducing learners to concepts that are difficult to present in text alone, or when it is difficult for the learner to experience a situation in real life.

If you develop digital content that can be reused, you may achieve the economies of scale necessary to sustain materials development and updating.

## Finding content and resources

You have three choices with regard to finding content to meet your session's learning outcomes:

1 Signpost existing content

2 Adapt existing face-to-face content or purchase off the shelf products

3 Create new content.

### Signposting existing content

There is an abundance of educational and learning materials available on the internet – sometimes too much! It can be time consuming to search websites and find appropriate materials to meet your learning outcomes. On the other hand, developing new content can be costly and just as time consuming. It is always worth checking whether what you want has been developed elsewhere, before creating new materials.

If you work for an educational or training provider, your organisation may have already set up a digital repository where the materials that other members of staff have produced or found are signposted. This repository could be on your provider's intranet or Virtual Learning Environment (VLE). If internal enquiries yield nothing, consider setting up an internal storage area for your resources so that others can add to it. Repositories can help improve the quality of the learning experience by making a wide selection of materials available for use, and therefore also cater for different learning styles.

If your organisation does not have an internal collection of learning resources, you may want to find out whether other members of staff have discovered any regional or national digital repositories. There are a number of higher education repositories, such as the SHERPA repository [http://www.sherpa.ac.uk/documents/rep_distrib.html], but these tend to be closed to users outside higher education, and the content may be research orientated. The Jorum collection of learning resources is currently aimed only at higher education and further education colleges [http://www.jorum.ac.uk/getstarted/index.html], so if you work for a college, you may be able to join this community.

If this fails, consider a search on the internet for the topic you hope to deliver.

The Joint Information Systems Committee (JISC) operates a series of regional offices that offer advice and guidance to key contacts in supporting learning providers. These JISC Regional Support Centres (RSCs) [http://www.jisc.ac.uk/whatwedo/services/as_rsc/rsc_home.aspx] may be able to point to resources you could use.

When looking for resources, try the following websites:

- The Quality Improvement Agency (QIA) Teaching and Learning Programme [http://teachingandlearning.qia.org.uk/teachingandlearning] website has links to curriculum-based resources. It includes not only subject content but other materials that can help you deliver a curriculum-based topic. The site points to resources for: society, health and development; construction and the built environment; engineering; creative and media; customer care; learning mathematics in context; IT; modern foreign languages; and many more.

- A national initiative, the NLN Materials [http://www.nln.ac.uk], produced high quality, multimedia, curriculum-based resources. The resources are freely available to some public-funded educational and training providers. Your organisation must be a registered user of the NLN materials to gain access. If you try to register as a new user, you will see which organisations qualify.

The NLN materials are well worth looking at and may meet your needs. The materials consist of small, self-contained learning activities that last about 15–20 minutes each. The activities are not whole courses but are designed to support a wide range of subject and topic areas. NLN materials specifically targeted at the community-based adult learning sector include content for family learning, modern foreign languages, making learning work for you, and English for Speakers of Other Languages (ESOL).

Materials can be accessed online or downloaded from the NLN website and either added to your learning platform or intranet or saved to a CD-ROM, DVD or removable storage device. Advice on downloading these resources and using them within the Moodle learning platform is available on the NLN website.

- The BBC has a range of short, focused learning objects, such as its online courses [http://www.bbc.co.uk/learning/onlinecourses], or WebWise [http://www.bbc.co.uk/webwise], aimed at people who are new to using the internet. If your aim is to encourage reading and writing and basic skills, look at the RaW (Reading and Writing) games [http://www.bbc.co.uk/raw/gamesandquizzes] and SkillsWise pages [http://www.bbc.co.uk/skillswise]. Finally, Bitesize for schools [http://www.bbc.co.uk/schools/gcsebitesize] may have something that you could signpost and contextualise for your courses for adults.

If your learners are extensive users of mobile phones and other mobile technologies, you may want to signpost resources within your online course that can be viewed on handheld devices. Suitable technologies range from MP3 players and mobile phones to super-lightweight laptops. Handheld technology is beginning to make the benefits of e-learning more portable and more widely available. Further information about the technology is available on the NIACE Handheld Technology website [http://www.niace.org.uk/mobiletechnology].

Once you have found relevant content, ensure that, when you integrate it into your learning session by signposting it, you provide the necessary information and guidance for your learners so that they know exactly what is expected of them and how to make use of the content. Also, if you are permitted to use the content only if you cite the source, make sure you add the relevant references within your course.

## Adapt existing face-to-face content or purchase off-the-shelf products

A number of tutors start by converting their paper-based resources into a digital format and making them available online. Although this is acceptable at first, if you do not have access to the skills or expertise to amend resources for online delivery, you will not make best use of the multimedia opportunities that online delivery can bring. Always try to start from the learner's point of view. Will making the materials available online without much adaptation achieve your learning aims? If not, explore what actions you need to take to make the materials more effective.

A number of commercial providers have developed digital content which can be purchased at a cost. You can place these materials on an internal network, intranet or VLE. You may find that you can either only use the resources in their current form, or, if you can amend them, restrictions may apply. Check out the copyright before you purchase any product.

If you search the internet and find relevant content, you may still need to modify it to suit your context and learners. First, find out whether the content's copyright allows you to use the resources and, more importantly, change them. Some materials are available for use only if no changes are made. You may also find that the authors will let you use materials so long as you cite the source (the website, publication or journal where you found the content). It is possible to find resources that are copyright free or for which the authors give permission for you to amend them.

Depending on the technology used to create the content, adapting it may require technical skill. Some content is easier to adapt than others. Complex resources, such as multimedia-rich learning objects, are best left to technical experts.

The types of software you may need in order to adapt materials depend on the content type, for example whether it is an audio or video clip, an image or a piece of animation.

Whatever you decide to do, if the digital resources you provide are not accessible to all users, you will need either to change them so that they are, or provide alternative methods for users in order to meet the intended learning outcomes. Legislation protects disabled learners by requiring learning providers to make appropriate provision. Accessibility is discussed in Chapter 2: 'Designing the learning space'.

A number of learning providers and organisations are beginning to encourage users to amend the content they have developed. For example, the Open University Open Learning initiative [http://openlearn.open.ac.uk/course/view.php?id=3416] in the UK and the Massachusetts Institute of Technology (MIT) [http://ocw.mit.edu/OcwWeb/web/home/home/index.htm] in the USA are making curriculum content available to the public and encouraging users to adapt it for their own use. NIACE provides a guide on how to use the Open University's resources in adult learning on its Moodle [http://moodle.niace.org.uk/moodle]; select **Login as a guest** and navigate to **OpenLearn from the Open University – Showcase**.

The nationally produced NLN Materials, mentioned previously, can also be customised. NIACE has produced a showcase on its Moodle that describes how you might adapt these resources for your curriculum [http://moodle.niace.org.uk/moodle]; select **Login as a guest** and navigate to **NLN Materials – Showcase**. The NLN Materials were created by commercial developers in partnership with subject matter experts and a wide range of colleges and adult and community learning experts. All the materials were trialed by tutors and students and tested for accessibility at the Royal National College of the Blind in Hereford, UK.

Curriculum resources specifically for use in adult learning can be found on the QIA website [http://www.qiaresources4adultlearning.net]. The resources form part of the QIA's guidance on improving teaching and learning in adult learning.

Finally, a number of commercial companies provide content, although you pay to use it. Once you have bought the content, you could make it available to learners via your learning platform. How you use these off-the-shelf resources depends on the copyright. Some of the products can be used only as they were created, while others can be amended only if they are used in certain contexts, such as for educational purposes. This could mean that the resources cannot be used within online courses for which a fee is charged.

## Create new content

It is worth considering creating your own content if you cannot find the right resources, you cannot amend existing resources because the copyright will not allow it, you do not have the appropriate level of technical expertise, or your subject content needs to be very specific to your circumstances.

You have two main choices when creating your own content:

- Enable practitioners and tutors to create their own resources.

- Form a team of individuals combining curriculum-specific knowledge with technical and other related skills.

*Practitioners doing it for themselves*

You can get a real sense of satisfaction from producing your own content. First, you can tailor the materials to your learners and therefore give them the best chance of achieving their learning aims. Secondly, you decide which tools to use and therefore can begin to develop content using software you are already familiar with, for example word processing and presentation software, or free software obtained via the internet. Finally, you can build up your technical skills slowly, starting from presenting simple text with images, through to creating multimedia-rich learning materials.

You can assess your current information and communications technology (ICT) competencies by using the Learning and Skills Network's ICT skills self-assessment tool [http://www.learningtechnologies.ac.uk/SA/default.asp]. The tool can be used as part of a staff continuing professional development (CPD) programme.

Those involved in content creation may want to consider collaborating with learners to create resources either before, during or after an online session. This is a powerful way of both involving learners in creating content for future online activities and engaging them more deeply in the learning process. Involving learners in the creation of resources is an interesting way to improve their IT skills and help them understand how to produce content for different audiences, while contributing to your resource bank. Make sure that you have the necessary permissions to use any resources created by learners within other sessions or courses.

For example, learners could use mobile phones with built-in sound recorders to record someone reading a short review of a book, which learners could then discuss. They could capture images on their mobile phones, around which a story could be created. Or maybe learners could develop simple spreadsheets that calculate household expenditure and income in a numeracy session; in the future, you could ask other learners to improve on the spreadsheet. You could even include learners in the design of the course and ask them to write or improve on the documentation for it.

Involving learners in the design of your courses and in your content creation has the potential to change the relationship between facilitator and learner. The process becomes a collaborative process where all those involved can benefit from the experience.

If you are using a VLE, find out whether it includes content creation tools that help you develop your own content. A number of these tools are simple to use and enable you to develop activities such as quizzes, simple linked web pages and surveys. Once created, you could store the materials within your VLE to be shared across other courses.

If a VLE is open source, other VLE users can create additional facilities for the environment and make them freely available via the internet. This has happened for the Moodle VLE: users of Moodle have created a strong online community; when people develop additional components that work within Moodle, they place them on the internet so that others can use them.

There are numerous sources of content creation help on the internet. The following is just a selection:

- The Staff development e-learning centre (SDELC) website includes advice aimed at post-16 education providers on using an assortment of content creation tools. Log in and go to **Tutor modules** > **E-learning content – sourcing and creating**. This section explores creating your own interactive content using generic software packages such as Microsoft® Office [http://office.microsoft.com/en-gb/default.aspx], Hot Potatoes™ [http://www.halfbakedsoftware.com/hot_pot.php], Wimba Create [http://www.wimba.com] and Microsoft Photo Story 3 [http://www.microsoft.com/windowsxp/using/digitalphotography/photostory/default.mspx]. Getting to grips with the tools covered in this section of the SDELC site will enable you to create a basic online session, event or course.

- The Learning and Skills Network (LSN) provides examples of content created using generic software and which is suited to the delivery of subject-specific ITQs [http://www.learningtechnologies.ac.uk/itqss]. (ITQ is the National Vocational Qualification for IT users.) The examples may give you ideas of the sorts of content that can be created by practitioners who have an understanding of generic software.

- The Joint Information Systems Committee Regional Support Centres (JISC RSCs) [http://www.jisc.ac.uk/rsc] also provide guidance on using technology in learning and teaching and some give advice on their websites on using certain tools and software. For example, the RSC Northern office [http://www.rsc-northern.ac.uk/learningandteaching/learningtechnologies] has guidance on creating podcasts. (Podcasts are audio broadcasts in a format that can be played on digital music players or through your computer.)

- University College London (UCL) has a section on creating content as part of its Learning Technology website [http://www.ucl.ac.uk/learningtechnology].

## Feedback and assessment

*'And while it is true that opportunities for learner feedback and formative assessment do not ensure that learning happens, their presence allows the learner to evaluate learning progress and they can also stimulate engagement.'*

Ken Allan, in a discussion paper on learning objects [http://www.futurelab.org.uk/resources/publications_reports_articles/discussion_papers/Discussion_Paper971]

It is important that, when considering the design of your online course or learning event and planning the content for it, you include opportunities for assessment and feedback – ie both assessment **for** learning as well as assessment **of** learning. Online assessments not only test understanding and knowledge (assessment of learning) but give instant feedback, provide opportunities to reinforce learning and increase learners' confidence (assessment for learning).

If your content is to be delivered in an asynchronous manner, in which learners can work at their own pace over a period, you may need to find out what learners already know – what areas of the course or event they have already covered – and how you will evaluate what individuals have learnt. You might do this by incorporating formative and summative assessments or by providing online or face-to-face human intervention along the way.

On the other hand, if you are delivering a synchronous session, you may want to build in ways of discovering whether your learners are paying attention, and obtaining feedback from them, during and maybe after the live session to check their understanding. Asynchronous and synchronous tools were covered in more detail in Chapter 2: 'Designing the learning space'.

Assessment of learning is a concept that most learning providers are familiar with. Traditional face-to-face courses often involve some method to collect evidence that learners have achieved the learning outcomes. For an online course or event, assessment of learning may involve designing question-and-answer sessions, setting assignments, giving learners tests to complete or conducting online debates.

A number of sources can help you in signposting to, amending or creating assessments to assist or evaluate learning:

- SDELC website [http://www.sdelc.org.uk]: This is the first port of call. Log in to the site; you can find information about how to use a range of software to create assessments in **Tutor modules > E-learning content – sourcing and creating**. The SDELC website also provides step-by-step guides on how to use Microsoft Word to create drag-and-drop activities, check box forms and comment boxes in assessments, and how you can use aspects of Microsoft PowerPoint® more interactively to engage learners. It also describes how to use Hot Potatoes™ to create short question-and-answer quizzes, gap-fill exercises, crosswords and drag-and-drop exercises, and provides guidance on using Wimba Create to create matching, multi-choice and multi-response exercises.

- RSC Northwest: This office provides a free web-based authoring tool that enables you to create simple quizzes. You can download the software from the RSC Northwest website [http://www.rsc-northwest.ac.uk/acl/BookCase/RSCWebBasedTest.exe] then follow the on-screen instructions.

- Crossword creation tools: As well as Hot Potatoes, a number of crossword creation tools are available via the internet. Crossword Compiler [http://www.crossword-compiler.com] and Crossword Creator [http://www.csfsoftware.co.uk/Crossword_info.htm] are two examples, but there are many others. Crosswords can help individuals to learn vocabulary, remember facts and prepare for formative tests or final examinations.

- Assessments and quizzes created by others: The internet is also a source of ready-made assessments and quizzes:

    o The HotPot Sites [http://hotpot.uvic.ca/sites6.htm] area of the Hot Potatoes website links to example sites and to ready-made quizzes.

    o Teach ICT [http://www.teach-ict.com/index.html] offers quizzes to help teach ICT skills.

○ Teachers Direct [http://www.teachers-direct.co.uk/resources] includes quizzes aimed at various curriculum areas.

○ BBC: Learning [http://www.bbc.co.uk/learning] and Bytesize [http://www.bbc.co.uk/schools/gcsebitesize] provide quizzes that could be contextualised for adult learners. BBC Learning English [http://www.bbc.co.uk/worldservice/learningenglish] offers more quizzes that could be adapted for adult learners.

- VLE tools: If you are using a VLE, it will undoubtedly include integrated tools for providing feedback and assessment.

Assessment for learning involves the same sorts of activities as those used for assessment of learning, but requires a few additional elements to engage and motivate learners. You should:

- provide the opportunity to reflect on progress and the learning process itself

- include activities that encourage peer learning and assessment: learners could create online multiple-choice quizzes for other learners, or mentor their peers to improve the self-reflection processes.

By placing learners at the centre of the assessment process, it is more likely they will take ownership of it.

### Pause and reflect

- How do you currently find materials for face-to-face delivery?

- What do you see as the challenges for team leaders and tutors who want to incorporate digital content into teaching and learning practice?

## Checklist: Your content

You can use this checklist to help you plan your online learning provision in your own organisation.

|  | Yes | No | Perhaps |
|---|---|---|---|
| **Where will my content come from?** | | | |
| Signposting to existing content | | | |
| Adapting existing face-to-face content | | | |
| Purchasing off the shelf products | | | |
| Creating new content | | | |
| **How will my new content be created?** | | | |
| By practitioners and tutors | | | |
| By technical experts with curriculum-specific knowledge | | | |
| A combination of practitioners and technical experts | | | |
| **Do I have systems in place for feedback and assessment?** | | | |
| Assessment for learning | | | |
| Assessment of learning | | | |

# Chapter 6:
# Quality assurance and control

This chapter explores the ways in which online provision can be quality assured.

There are numerous definitions of quality. Harman and Meek (2000) define quality assurance as '*systematic management and assessment procedures… to ensure achievement of quality outputs or improved quality*'. The American Society for Quality (ASQ) states '*Quality denotes an excellence in goods and services, especially to the degree they conform to requirements and satisfy customers.*' Derived from the manufacturing industry, fitness for purpose is an assessment of a product against its stated purpose – the need here is to conform to generally accepted standards. Anderson, Johnson and Milligan (2000) warn against '*focusing too much on processes and not enough on academic standards and outcomes*' in quality assurance plans.

Yet, none of these definitions gets to the heart of the complex, interactive process that is learning. These definitions appear to overlook the value of learning and the nature of our education system. Perhaps a learner-centred approach is about providing opportunities for individuals to:

- operate as lifelong learners who can communicate effectively

- access information and think critically

- act as productive members of society.

This more learner-centred approach does not negate the economic needs of society, but it does put the learner firmly at the heart of the process. Poor quality makes it difficult for individuals to learn – it could leave learners not wanting to learn, or convinced that they cannot learn. NIACE's online courses adopt a learner-centred approach to quality.

According to the Online Tutoring Skills (OTIS) website [http://otis.scotcit.ac.uk], quality assurance of learning starts with design and continues through delivery, on to feedback and finally to review. OTIS suggests that you can approach this cyclic process from four different perspectives:

1 Organisational (infrastructure and technology tools, administration)

2 Course level (curriculum team, faculty, department)

3 Session level (module, unit, session, chunk of learning)

4 Individual (the experience of the learner).

Each perspective is discussed below.

## Organisational

If you work for an adult-learning provider, it is likely that your organisation will already have in place a quality assurance process for your face-to-face delivery. Sometimes, such processes are to satisfy external inspection processes or funders' needs; at other times, they are to satisfy internal quality improvement requirements.

At organisational level, any quality system you put into place needs to take account of the amount of learning achieved relative to the resources invested. Your quality processes need to be supported by a robust technical infrastructure and ease of access to equipment, systematic monitoring procedures, internal and external verification and accreditation processes, regular learner and facilitator feedback, ongoing staff support and development, and the sharing of good practice. Evaluation forms the core of a successful quality assurance strategy.

If you are unclear what your quality criteria should be for your online learning provision or how quality assurance can fit into your existing quality practices, consider undertaking research across your organisation to establish the following: your organisation's needs, the expectations of your learners, and the views of your tutors and support staff with regard to online learning provision.

## Course level

When developing or updating courses, adult learning providers often form a curriculum team to develop and design courses.

There are a number of conflicting pressures on curriculum design: external drivers such as central and local government policy and the need to create and maintain a market for courses and, of course, develop your learners. Often, the courses that emerge are a consequence of compromises as providers try to navigate the contradictory demands.

Online provision needs to form a part of the curriculum design process, although online developments require additional understanding of delivery technologies, the internet and web design (see Chapter 3: 'Developing online provision'). By integrating online delivery into the curriculum design processes at course level, you can extend the course quality processes already in place for face-to-face delivery to include online provision.

RMIT University in Australia has been developing online courses for some years. Most of its online provision supports blended delivery. The university has put in place a quality assurance plan for all its online activities. Before course development begins, staff present an outline of the course design showing how the use of technology will achieve the desired learning outcomes. Once the course has been developed, and before it can go live, a peer review process is undertaken. Tutors and facilitators comment on their colleagues' courses using a set of peer review criteria (see below).

## Peer review criteria

- The course ensures that learners are aware, from the start, of what is expected of them in terms of time commitment, engagement and assessment.

- At all times, learners know what activities and tasks to undertake.

- The skills, knowledge and experiences of learners were considered when developing the learning activities, assessments and resources.

- Learners undertaking the learning activities (including assessment) are likely to achieve the course's learning outcomes.

- The course's learning outcomes are explicitly incorporated in learning and assessment activities.

- The course meets the needs, wants and circumstances of the diversity of the anticipated learners, including addressing issues of equity of access.

- The course's level of language is suited to the learners.

- The course actively encourages and supports learner engagement and interaction.

- The assessment activities result in a judgement about whether the learner has met the desired learning outcomes.

- The course provides opportunities to give regular, constructive feedback to learners.

- The course provides opportunities for learners to provide feedback to the facilitators and course team leader throughout the course.

- Learners can readily locate and access all resources when needed.

- Learners know how to submit material to their peers or facilitators.

- The teaching and learning activities, including facilitator interventions, are reviewed and updated to maintain or enhance the quality of the course.

Adapted from: Quality assurance for online courses: from policy to process to improvement? McNaught, C. (2001), in Kennedy, G., Keppell, M., McNaught, C., Petrovic, T. (eds), Meeting at the Cross-roads, Proceedings of the 18th Annual Australian Society for Computers in Learning in Tertiary Education 2001 Conference, University of Melbourne, http://www.ascilite.org.au/conferences/melbourne01/pdf/papers/mcnaughtc.pdf

You can run elements of the quality assurance and peer review process online.

The most common issues identified in weak online courses were:

- failing to link resources and activities to learning outcomes

- lack of flexibility in catering for diverse groups of learners

- no links to activities; only the provision of resources and no guidance on using these resources

- a wide array of clickable buttons that were often confusing

- unclear navigation within the course.

Evidence from RMIT's experiences suggests the following overarching strategies for ensuring quality of online courses:

- Collect evidence that the course has gone through a clear educational design and planning process before it goes live.

- Enable facilitators to peer review the course before it starts. (A list of possible peer review criteria is suggested below.)

- Survey all potential learners at the start about their access to technology and their technology skills.

- Survey all potential learners at the start about their experience of online learning.

- Obtain regular feedback from learners about their perceptions of the online learning activities and tools, and of their access to – and use of – online resources.

- Obtain regular feedback from learners about their perceptions of the relationship between what they are currently doing within their course and other parts of the course – ie explore their ability to reflect on how the current session contributes to the learning objectives of the overarching course.

- Obtain regular feedback from learners about their perceptions of the levels of support they are receiving – technical, administrative and educational – and the effectiveness of any online communication.

- Use assessment results to provide evidence of areas of the course that learners can cope with and areas that they find challenging.

- Ensure that time is built in to the course at the end for review and for any amendments to be made to the course.

These strategies align well with the processes that NIACE has employed in quality assuring its online provision. NIACE also includes, as part of its quality process, opportunities for facilitators to undertake peer observations online. These observations enable facilitators to help each other improve their online facilitation skills. Fortunately, many online tools enable you to record facilitator and learner inputs automatically, therefore providing some of the evidence you need to meet your quality criteria.

It may also help if you establish an online space for facilitators. Facilitators who want to discuss problems and successes, obtain technical support or disseminate good practice can then use these online discussion areas. Online discussion facilities can also support peer review sessions, in which members of staff comment on and discuss each other's partially or fully developed online sessions or courses.

The NIACE Online Course Delivery project has a dedicated facilitator's area – a virtual staff room – within its Moodle environment. This is a private area accessible only to the facilitators and certain team members for the project. A wide range of issues and topics are discussed within this area, and there is also space for online social interactions. For our learners, we have a 'graduating class' area to enable peer support and networking to continue after learners have completed the course. Facilitators and learners who choose to join this area do so on an equal footing.

## Session level (module, unit, section, chunk of learning)

By including an evaluation activity for learners at the end of each session, you can gather vital evidence to feed in to your quality assurance. An end-of-session evaluation is one way of assessing how successful the session was in meeting its objectives and the overall aim of the course.

At the session level, the types of issues you may address include the:

- relevance of the session's learning objectives to learners
- ability of the session to maintain interest
- ease of navigation through the session
- number and appropriateness of any interactive activities
- amount and appropriateness of the support provided
- appropriate use of assessment for learning (feedback as a mechanism to improve knowledge, learning and skills)
- appropriate use of assessment of learning (to find out whether learners have achieved the intended learning outcomes).

Do not forget, also, to provide facilitators with an opportunity to reflect on the session. Giving them a chance to note down their thoughts – either individually or as a group – about their interventions with learners and experiences with the course provides you with valuable feedback in the next cycle of course development and can contribute to the personal development of facilitators.

## Individual (the experience of the learner)

A popular way of gaining learner feedback on sessions is to ask for learners' immediate reactions and attitudes on completion. It is important that you give learners the opportunity to reflect on the learning process itself, in addition to assessing what they have learnt. You could ask learners' thoughts and feelings in relation to the following:

- their levels of engagement

- their levels of interest

- areas of the learning process they found challenging and those they found easier to manage

- what went well and what might have gone better.

You can obtain this feedback through, for example:

- online methods, such as:

  o online evaluation forms, sometimes knows as 'happy sheets'

  o reflective diaries or blogs, which can be submitted as email attachments if you are not using a VLE with built-in facilities

  o questionnaires or surveys using web-based forms

  o interviewing individual learners in a chat session or by instant message or email

○ holding an online feedback session for all learners.

- observation of the session by an experienced facilitator to gauge learner engagement

- interviewing individual learners face to face or by phone.

Learner engagement and feedback is important, not only at the end of a learning activity or course, but throughout the course design, development and delivery process.

### Pause and reflect

- How would you advise an adult learning provider who wanted to integrate its online provision within its existing quality assurance procedures?

## Checklist: Your quality assurance

You can use this checklist to help you plan your online learning provision in your own organisation.

|  | Yes | No | Perhaps |
|---|---|---|---|
| **Have I considered quality assurance from all perspectives?** | | | |
| Organisational | | | |
| Course level | | | |
| Session level | | | |
| Individual | | | |
| **How will I gather evaluative data?** | | | |
| Evaluation forms | | | |
| Reflective diaries or blogs | | | |
| Questionnaires | | | |
| Surveys | | | |
| Interviews | | | |
| Group feedback session | | | |

# Conclusion

So many aspects of our lives today involve communicating using online methodologies. As many people now log on to license their cars, check their bank accounts and keep in touch with friends, it is not surprising that we are interested in learning online as well.

As it becomes easier and cheaper to access the internet, and more software tools become available, the opportunities for online learning are exciting, but the wide range of choices can also be daunting for an adult learning provider planning to move into this area. In this publication, we have tried to help providers make sense of these choices by describing the landscape of online learning and pointing to the questions that any learning organisation needs to consider before developing online learning courses and opportunities.

Online learning can help us learn at different times and wherever we happen to be. It can also offer a greater variety of ways to learn, including learning from each other. The collaborative nature of emerging social software (software that enables learners to be co-creators and shapers of learning content and other resources) brings with it a real opportunity to shift the balance of power between those who in the past have delivered education and training and those who have been the recipients of it.

The key messages from this publication are that an organisational and strategic approach to online courses and delivery is more likely to result in online provision becoming a part of an adult learning provider's formal and informal learning provision. It moves away from a dependency on purely localised, ad-hoc online developments initiated by one or two enthusiastic individuals and towards a more systematic approach to online developments.

Staff skills, technical infrastructure and good marketing are all important elements of any online learning strategy, but at the heart of the success of your online learning project is the use of good methods of teaching and learning, provided in the ways that your learners really do want. This means involving learners at all stages of the process from inception, through course design, to assessment and quality assurance. In this way, there is a stronger chance that not only will your learners arrive at their intended destination, but that they have a voice in transforming the delivery of learning.

# Further information/references

Anderson, D., Johnson, R. and Milligan, B. (2000). Quality assurance and accreditation in Australian higher education: An assessment of Australian and international practice, Evaluations and Investigations Programme report 00/1, Department of Education, Training and Youth Affairs, Australia.
http://www.dest.gov.au/archive/highered/eippubs/eip00_1/fullcopy00_1.pdf (accessed 29 August 2008)

Berge, Z.L. (1995). The role of the online instructor/facilitator, on the eModerators website,
http://www.emoderators.com/moderators/teach_online.html (accessed 29 August 2008)

Chen, S. (2002). A cognitive model of non-linear learning in hypermedia programs, *British Journal of Educational Technology*, 33(4), 449–460.

Daniels, H.L. and Moore, D.M. (2000). Interaction of cognitive style and learner control in a hypermedia environment, *International Journal of Instructional Media*, 27(4), 369–382.

Dede, C. (1996). The evolution of distance education: Emerging technologies and distributed learning, *The American Journal of Distance Education*, 10(2), 4–36.

Ford, N. and Chen, Y. (2000). Individual differences, hypermedia navigation and learning: An empirical study, *Journal of Educational Multimedia and Hypermedia*, 9(4), 281–311.

Harman, G. and Meek, V.L. (2000). Repositioning quality assurance and accreditation in Australian higher education, Evaluations and Investigations Programme report 00/2, Department of Education, Training and Youth Affairs, Australia.
http://www.dest.gov.au/archive/highered/eippubs/eip00_2/fullcopy00_2.pdf (accessed 29 August 2008)

Hislop, G. (2000) Working professionals as part-time on-line learners, Journal of Asynchronous Learning Networks, 4(2).
http://www.sloan-c-wiki.org/JALN/v4n2/pdf/v4n2_hislop.pdf (accessed 05 September 2008)

Kearsley, G. (2000). Learning and teaching in cyberspace, http://home.sprynet.com/~gkearsley/chapts.htm

King, K.P. (1998). Course development on the World Wide Web, in Cahoon, B., Adult learning and the internet: New directions for adult and continuing education (vol. 78), **http://www.georgiacenter.uga.edu/idl/internet/development.html** (accessed 18 July 2008)

Knowles, M.S. (1980). *The modern practice of adult education: From pedagogy to andragogy*, Chicago: Follett.

Knowles, M.S. (1984). *Andragogy in action*, San Francisco: Jossey-Bass.

Mayes, T. and de Freitas, S. (2007). JISC e-Learning Models Desk Study, Stage 2: Review of e-learning theories, frameworks and models, JISC. **http://www.jisc.ac.uk/uploaded_documents/Stage%202%20Learning%20Models%20(Version%201).pdf**

Oh, E. and Lim, D. (2005) Cross relationships between cognitive styles and learner variables in online learning environment, J*ournal of Interactive Online Learning*, 4(1) summer, **http://www.ncolr.org/jiol/issues/PDF/4.1.4.pdf** (accessed 13 June 2008)

Palloff, R.M. and Pratt, K. (1999). *Building learning communities in cyberspace*, San Francisco: Jossey-Bass.

# Appendices

## Appendix A: Learning styles

**Kolb learning style inventory (LSI)**: The Kolb inventory identifies two types of learning activity: perception and processing. The model is based on the view that an individual perceives new information on a continuum from concrete to abstract, and processes what is perceived on a continuum from active to reflective (Kolb, 2000). The model consists of four aspects – diverging, assimilating, converging, and accommodating – that reflect the two processing and perception continua. More information about the aspects can be found on the ChangingMinds.org website
**[http://changingminds.org/explanations/learning/kolb_learning.htm]**.

**Honey and Mumford learning styles questionnaire**: This model was developed by Peter Honey and Alan Mumford from Kolb's learning inventory and consists of four learning styles: activists (prefer to learn by doing), reflectors (like to sit back, observe and reflect) pragmatists (like to leap in and act) and theorists (prefer to fit everything into neat systems/plans). Given that the model arose from Kolb's inventory, there are some similarities between Honey and Mumford's and Kolb's learning styles. An explanation of the categories and their relationship to e-tutoring can be found on Richard Mobbs' (University of Leicester) website
**[http://www.le.ac.uk/cc/rjm1/etutor/resources/learningtheories/honeymumford.html]**.

**Index of Learning Styles**: Felder and Silverman's Index of Learning Styles (revised in 2002) suggests four dimensions of learning styles: active (prefer to act)/reflective (prefer to reflect), sensing (like to learn facts)/intuitive (prefer to explore concepts and relationships), visual (remember best what they see)/verbal (remember best what is written or heard), and sequential (gain understanding in linear steps)/global (learn in large steps to grasp the bigger picture). You can try the index out for yourself by filling in a questionnaire and receiving immediate feedback on the North Carolina State University website **[http://www4.ncsu.edu/unity/lockers/users/f/felder/public/ILSpage.html]**. This website also provides helpful suggestions on how you can learn better, given your preferred learning style.

**Visual, auditory, kinaesthetic (VAK)**: This theory proposes three main preferences: visual (preference for seeing and reading), auditory (preference for listening and speaking) or kinaesthetic (preference for touching and doing). According to the VAK model, most people have a preferred learning

style, while some people prefer a mix of the three styles. You can find out more about this approach at
**[http://honolulu.hawaii.edu/intranet/committees/FacDevCom/guidebk/teachtip/vark.htm]**.

**Multiple intelligences**: This approach is based on the work of Howard Gardner. Intelligence is categorised into eight areas: verbal linguistic (the ability to use words and language); logical mathematical (a highly developed ability to use reason, logic and numbers); bodily kinaesthetic (the capacity to control body movement and handle physical objects); visual spatial (a strong visual capacity to think in pictures and create pictures in the mind); musical rhythmical (a heightened ability to appreciate and produce music and sound); interpersonal (the advanced ability to relate to and understand other people); intrapersonal (the presence of a strong sense of self and ability to understand and share inner thoughts and feelings); and naturalist (a recognition, appreciation and understanding of the natural world around us). Gardner's website contains further information
**[http://www.howardgardner.com/MI/mi.html]**.

# Appendix B: Accessibility websites

### UK

Disability Discrimination Act 1995, 1999 (DDA) – see the Directgov website [http://www.direct.gov.uk/en/DisabledPeople/index.htm] and the Office of Public Sector Information website **[http://www.opsi.gov.uk/acts/acts1995/ukpga_19950050_en_1]**.

Disability Rights Commission Act 1999 – see the Office of Public Sector Information website **[http://www.opsi.gov.uk/acts/acts1999/ukpga_19990017_en_1]**.

Special Education Needs and Disability Act 2001 (SENDA) – see the Office of Public Sector Information website **[http://www.opsi.gov.uk/ACTS/acts2001/ukpga_20010010_en_1]**.

TechDis website **[http://www.techdis.ac.uk]**.

### America

Americans with Disabilities Act 1990, 1995 (ADA) – see the ADA website **[http://www.ada.gov]**.

Section 508 of the US Rehabilitation Act 1986, amended 1998 – see the ADA website **[http://www.usdoj.gov/crt/508/508home.html]**.

Workforce Investment Act 1998 – see the US Department of Labor website **[http://www.doleta.gov/USWORKFORCE/WIA/act.cfm]**.

### Australia

Disability Discrimination Act 1992 – see the Australasian Legal Information Institute website **[http://www.austlii.edu.au/au/legis/cth/consol_act/dda1992264]**.

Australian disability standards and guidelines – see the Human Rights and Equal Opportunity Commission website **[http://www.hreoc.gov.au/disability_rights/standards/standards.html]**.

New South Wales Anti-Discrimination Act 1977 – see the Australasian Legal Information Institute website **[http://www.austlii.edu.au/au/legis/nsw/consol_act/aa1977204]**.

### Canada:

Canadian Human Rights Act 1985 – see the Department of Justice Canada website **[http://laws.justice.gc.ca/en/H-6/relprov.html]**.

# Appendix C: Example of time taken by NIACE for initial course creation and delivery

This example is based on NIACE's experiences in creating, from scratch, a ten-week, level-3-accredited online course, mostly text-based, involving 20 learners and two facilitators, which includes an optional face-to-face induction day.

| Course creation | | No of days |
|---|---|---|
| Project manager (PM)/team leader | Identify project team. Develop and communicate concept. Identify and recruit content authors. Identify/review existing materials/links to be used. Prepare for and brief project team and content authors. Review materials from content authors. Identify and recruit facilitators. Prepare for and brief/induct facilitators. | 22 |
| Project officer (PO) | Support PM, as directed, in above tasks. Perform editing/consistency work on materials. Oversee conversion of materials to online format. Create course area and facilitator support area. Develop course handbook and guides for learners and facilitators. Place course materials and any facilitator support materials on the learning platform. | 22 |
| Administrator | Support PM and PO, as directed, in above tasks. | 4 |
| Technical | Convert materials to online format. Carry out technical set-up requirements for learning platform. Set up course area and place materials and activities onto the delivery system (learning platform). | 16 |
| | | **64 days total** |

| Course delivery | | No of days |
|---|---|---|
| Printer/administrator – handbooks | Produce handbooks, guides for facilitators and learners, and internal course completion certificates. | 1 |
| Facilitation (includes meetings) | Provide course facilitation and personal tutor support for duration of course. Provide feedback during course evaluation. Respond to additional requests from PM and PO. Attend meetings and induction as directed by PM. | 30 |
| Project officer (support, evaluation) | Support facilitators. Oversee accreditation. Manage project paper trail and budget. Provide technical support. (1 day per week of course.) | 10 |
| Administration | Support PO in above tasks. Arrange meetings. Despatch handbooks, etc. (Half a day per week of course.) | 5 |
| Accreditation administration | Handle accreditation registration and paper trail. Prepare for and attend verification meetings. Despatch certificates. | 4 |
| | | **50 days total** |

# Appendix D: Example assessment and tracking sheet for learners

## Assessment and tracking sheet
## Module 1: Exploring online learning

| Unit | Task | | Done |
|---|---|---|---|
| | Module aims and objectives | Reading material | ❏ |
| Section 1 | Introduction to section | Reading material | ❏ |
| | Previous online learning | Reading material | ❏ |
| | | Discussion forum: Previous online learning | ❏ |
| | Exploring an online course | Reading material | ❏ |
| | | Complete short online course | ❏ |
| | | Discussion forum: Exploring new courses | ❏ |
| | Summary | Reading material | ❏ |
| Section 2 | Introduction to section | Reading material | ❏ |
| | Target audience for online delivery methods | Reading material | ❏ |
| | | Assignment: Target audience | ❏ |
| | Five types of online learning | Reading material – presentation | ❏ |
| | | Assignment: Types of online learning | ❏ |
| | | Discussion forum: Uses of online learning | ❏ |
| | Summary | Reading material | ❏ |

# Appendix E: Acceptable use policy for the NIACE Moodle

### Site user policy

When you register on the NIACE Moodle website, you are asked to confirm your acceptance of the notice boards and discussion group standards and the discussion groups and notice board rules. These are also shown below:

### Notice boards and discussion group standards

Your privilege to use and contribute to discussions depends on your compliance with the **Discussion Group and Notice Board Rules** ('the **Rules**').

NIACE may take appropriate measures to enforce the **Rules** if violations are brought to its attention. NIACE reserves the right to delete any posting at any time for any reason.

If you fail to abide by the **Rules** you will be formally warned by email. If after any warning you continue to breach the **Rules** you will be prohibited from using the discussion groups and notice boards. However NIACE reserves the right to terminate your access to the discussion groups and notice boards at any time without notice for any reason whatsoever.

You agree to use the discussion groups and notice boards only to send and receive messages and material that are proper and related to the particular forum.

NIACE has no obligation to monitor the discussion groups and notice boards but reserves the right at all times to disclose any information as necessary to satisfy any applicable law, regulation or legal process or refuse to post any information or materials, in whole or in part.

The materials are not edited for content, style or errors. You are responsible and liable for all activities conducted through your use of the discussion groups and notice boards.

### Discussion groups and notice board rules

By using the NIACE discussion groups and notice boards you agree not to engage in any of the following acts:

Defame, abuse, harass, threaten or in any other way violate the legal rights of others.

Post vulgar, obscene, sexually explicit or racially abusive material or adopt an inappropriate user name.

Post any illegal material of any nature including text, graphics, video, audio or programs.

Post any material including text, graphics, video, audio or programs with the intention of committing an illegal act.

Post any materials including text, graphics, video, audio or programs to which you do not own the copyright or other necessary consents to distribute electronically or distribute such material which is protected by intellectual property laws or by rights of privacy.

Post any material including text, graphics, video, audio or programs which may plagiarise or infringe on the rights of third parties.

Download any file posted by another user that you know, or reasonably ought to know, cannot be legally distributed in such a manner.

Post or transmit any unsolicited advertising, promotional materials, or any form of solicitation or offer to sell any goods or services for any commercial purpose.

Impersonate any person, body corporate or other form of organisation or institution.

Upload files that contain viruses, corrupted files, or any other similar software or programs that may damage the operation of another's computer.

Falsify or delete any author's contributions, legal or other notices or proprietary designations or labels of the origin or source of software or any other material contained in a file that is uploaded to the discussion groups and notice boards.

You acknowledge that all discussion groups and notice boards are public communications and may be read by others without your knowledge.

By posting messages, uploading files, inputting data or engaging in any other form of communication through the discussion groups and notice boards you are granting NIACE permission to use, modify, copy, distribute, transmit, publicly display, reproduce, publish or sell any such communication.

NIACE reserves the right to edit or remove any content from a NIACE Moodle website should the content be deemed inappropriate.

**Netiquette**

Netiquette is network etiquette, the do's and don'ts of online communication. As with other forms of communication, some common courtesies should be followed.

*Discussion forum netiquette*

The basics of netiquette are agreed worldwide. Here are some points to consider when using a discussion forum (some points are also relevant to other forms of online communication):

- When you post a message, ensure that your message is relevant to the whole group, as each person reading it will spend some time doing so. Sometimes it is more appropriate to reply off list, using the person's email address, than to reply to the whole group.

- Focus on one topic per message. People often read only the first few lines of an email and, if the first topic does not interest them, they may not read the next topic in your message.

- Always include a relevant subject title for the message. This way people can immediately see whether the message is of interest.

- Avoid writing messages using all caps. IT LOOKS LIKE YOU'RE SHOUTING.

- Keep paragraphs and messages short and to the point. Long messages take up more bandwidth. Remember that some people pay for their internet access by the hour, so the longer it takes to read your messages, the more it costs.

*Flaming*

Sometimes you might offend someone unintentionally. Be prepared to receive some angry email or to be treated rudely in a public discussion. This is called being 'flamed'. If you attack back, you will spark a flame war. To contain the heat, the best response usually is no response at all.

*Message content*

Treat your messages as you would a postcard, bearing in mind that many people may read them. Cite all quotations, references and so on. Do not include personal or confidential information and be aware of copyright issues. Be professional and careful about what you say about others – your text is on public display and can be easily copied and forwarded. Libel laws still apply in cyberspace.

*Respect and confidentiality*

As part of the course, you will be working online in groups and engaging in discussions with managers and practitioners from other organisations. To allow open and honest communication and debate, all discussions on the forums and in online chat should be treated as confidential. You should not discuss the content with anyone outside the course without the express permission of the originator.

When working online, it is sometimes hard to remember that you are dealing with other human beings. At all times, treat others on the course with the same respect you would in a face-to-face discussion.

## Smileys

It is easy to misinterpret a message when you cannot see the communicator's body language. Bear this in mind, both when reading messages and writing them.

If you mean something to be humorous, use a smiley to indicate this. Smileys – also known as emoticons – are expressions you create from the characters on your keyboard. They add humour and personality to your messages. While these are not usually appropriate for professional emails, they can contribute a lot to more informal messages.

A few popular smileys include:

:-) Happy

:-e Disappointed

:-( Sad

:-< Mad

:-o Surprised

:-D Laughing

:-@ Screaming

;-) Winking

:-I Indifferent

When reading messages, do not assume someone is being rude or offensive. If you feel offended by another contribution, you should email the originator (off discussion) and explain how and why you feel offended.

## Further information

The above suggestions are based on:

Rinaldi, A., The net: User guidelines and netiquette, [http://courses.cs.vt.edu/~cs3604/lib/Netiquette/Rinaldi].

# Appendix F: Guidelines for facilitating online chat sessions

The following example is guidance provided to facilitators in the NIACE Online Course Delivery project.

**Facilitating online chat**

*Timing*

When organising a chat session, try to find a time convenient to the majority of participants – most of whom will have full-time jobs. Publicise your agreed times. Each session should be limited to about 45 minutes.

Co-facilitate early chat sessions – sessions can be particularly demanding when people are getting used to using the chat facility.

*Group size*

Try to limit group chats to between five and ten participants to give everyone an opportunity to participate.

*Provide opportunities for participation*

To ensure that as many people take part as possible, you could consider the following:

*Use a virtual seating plan*

A virtual seating plan would need to be provided to participants in advance of the session. Working around the table in the order of the seating plan, each participant is then asked to contribute.

- **Advantages**: Gives everyone an opportunity to speak; facilitator can concentrate on content, not on who has participated.

- **Disadvantages**: May put some participants under pressure to speak when they would rather not or have no point to make.

*Assign a character to indicate that a participant wants to speak*

A character – such as a question mark or asterisk – could be used to indicate, when typed, that the participant wants to speak.

- **Advantages**: Alerts the facilitator to participants who want to speak and are slower at typing, gives responsibility back to the learner, and means that the facilitator does not try to include someone with nothing to say.

- **Disadvantages**: Could be confusing and make the chat disjointed if used too often.

### Provide ground rules and/or rules of engagement

The ground rules should remind participants to treat people with the same courtesy that they would face to face, by not hogging the conversation. However, as with any conversation, some people prefer to talk and others to listen. Set a discussion topic to encourage participants to come up with ideas for the ground rules.

### General tips

- Make the chat activity purposeful and provide clear instructions – no-one will speak if they are unsure what the purpose of the activity is.

- Make sure participants know what to expect of the environment. Recommend that anyone who has not taken part in an online chat before tries to meet up with another participant to practise using the technology before taking part in a group chat.

- Provide preparatory information to participants to give them time to think of points they would like to make.

- Tackle poor behaviour in the chat room. As with discussion forums, any statements that contravene the site user policy should be dealt with immediately.

- Use cues to quieten someone who is talking too much – for example 'does anyone else want to comment on that point?'

- Remember how intimidating a chat room will be to some participants: it is the equivalent of being thrown into a room full of people who you do not really know and being expected to make intelligent conversation with them. Add to that a possible lack of knowledge about the technology and you have a recipe for anxiety for at least some of your participants.

- Consider how participants with more reflective learning styles will feel. Chat can become fast and furious if people are engaged with the content. Those who like to ponder the subject before making their point will find the conversation has moved on by the time they are ready to contribute.

- Ask participants to evaluate their experience in the chat room in their online reflective journal and ask for suggestions on how future chat sessions could be improved.

## Appendix G: Contact record sheet

The following example is from the NIACE Online Course Delivery project, and is provided before the start of the course both electronically and in hard copy as part of the handbook for facilitators.

### Contact record sheet

**Course name:** ........................ **Facilitator's name:** ...........................

| Date/ time | Participant's name | Issue | Feedback given |
|---|---|---|---|
|  |  |  |  |
|  |  |  |  |
|  |  |  |  |
|  |  |  |  |
|  |  |  |  |